ABOUT THE AUTHOR

Dr. Jesse Jai McNeil has served as pastor of the Tabernacle Baptist Church, Detroit, Michigan, since 1947, and prior to that time he served as pastor in New York and Nashville, Tennessee, and as Dean, School of Religion, Bishop College, Marshall, Texas. He received his B.S., M.A. and Ed.D. degrees from Columbia University and Union Theological Seminary in New York City. He also earned a Certificate in Ecumenical Studies at the Ecumenical Institute, Celigny, Switzerland, and the B.D. degree at Virginia Union University, School of Religion, Richmond. He has engaged in three travel and study missions for the World Council of Churches in Europe and has served a Consultant at the Second Assembly of the World Council of Churches at Evanston, Illinois, in 1954.

MINISTER'S SERVICE BOOK FOR PULPIT AND PARISH

Also by the author:

As Thy Days, So Thy Strength

Minister's Service Book
For Pulpit and Parish

◆ ◆ ◆

by
JESSE JAI McNEIL

William B. Eerdmans Publishing Company
Grand Rapids, Michigan

PREFACE

This book is the humble effort of one pastor to bring together under one cover and in convenient size the essential forms and orders and other aids of which he has found himself in frequent need in the more than twenty years he has served a free and non-liturgical Church. It contains nowhere in its pages any service or order which is sacrosanct.

All the materials in this book are meant to be instructive and suggestive. A minister may freely appropriate them in their present form and wording or in a similar form and wording. They are arranged in seven sections with a brief statement on Guiding Principles and Practical Suggestions introducing each. Each brief introductory statement seeks to set the material of that particular section in its proper theological and situational context so that the minister who uses this book may be aided in protecting himself from the perils of routine and rote.

While all the materials appearing in this book are for the most part the work of the author, he does not claim any originality in what he has done. He acknowledges his indebtedness to many sources, known and unknown to him; phrases, expressions and even ideas in a work of this nature are so unconsciously blended with one's own through years of constantly using various service books that the willing task of making proper and full acknowledgment of one's debt becomes a very arduous, if not an impossible one. Beyond the adaptation of certain portions from the Wedding and Burial Services of the *Book of Common Prayer,* editions certified in 1892, 1911, and 1945, the author has not intentionally appropriated any parts of other works of this nature. Yet because of the extensive use he has made during his parish ministry of certain sources of material — hence their influence upon him — he acknowledges his indebtedness to the following works: *A New Directory for the Public Worship of God,* prepared by a committee of the Public Worship Association of the (then) Free Church of Scotland, MacNiven and Wallace, 1898; *The Star Book for Ministers,* Edward T. Hiscox, the Judson Press, 1906; the *Book of Common Worship,* the Board of Christian Education of the Presbyterian Church in the U.S.A., 1932 and 1946 editions; and *The Pastor's Vade Mecum,* arranged by Leon Kurtz Williams, the Methodist Book Concern, 1933.

For all Scriptures used in this book and Scriptural expressions used in the prayers appearing herein, the author has relied upon the King James Version of the Holy Bible.

The author wishes to express his gratitude to Mrs. Lois Rowlett, for her faithful and competent assumption of the tedious and sometimes monotonous task of typing the manuscript. A number of his yokefellows in the parish ministry read either parts or all of the manuscript and offered helpful suggestions for its improvement. For this also he is humbly grateful.

He further acknowledges the constant and growing debt he owes to his wife, Pearl — a pastor's boon and indefatigable sharer of his yoke. Her help in the preparation of this book has been invaluable and his debt to her is beyond liquidation.

It is prayerfully hoped that this book will prove of some practical value to the pastor for whom it has been prepared and, especially, to the young minister who must rely upon some pattern by which he may render an acceptable and effective service to God and the people to whom he has been appointed a shepherd.

— JESSE JAI McNEIL

CONTENTS

7

10   Contents

For Those Seeking Forgiveness 159
For the Aged 163
For Those Who Have Recovered 166
For Those Who Face Death 168
Administration of The Lord's Supper for the Sick and
    Shut-In 169

Section Seven:

PRAYERS FOR VARIOUS NEEDS AND SPECIAL
    OCCASIONS 172
Guiding Principles and Practical Suggestions 172
Morning Prayers 173
Evening Prayers 174
Prayers of Thanksgiving 175
Prayers of Confession 176
Prayers of Petition 178
Prayers for Special Use 181
Prayers for Special Days 188

Section Eight:

A YEAR OF SCRIPTURE READINGS 196
Readings for January through December 197
Readings for the Lord's Supper 209
Readings for Youth Sunday 209
Readings for Palm Sunday 210
Readings for Good Friday 210
Readings for Easter Sunday 211
Readings for Pentecost Sunday 211
Readings for Thanksgiving Day 212
Readings for Christmas Day 212
Readings for Watch Night 212

The Public Worship of God

Morning and Evening Worship Services

GUIDING PRINCIPLES AND PRACTICAL SUGGESTIONS

Public worship is the public ascription of worth to God, the Father of our Lord and Saviour Jesus Christ, on the part of baptized believers whom He, through Christ Jesus, has called out of darkness into the marvelous light. It is the corporate response of these believers to His presence, His goodness, and His revelations through the Holy Word.

The public worship of God should be characterized by order as a necessary element in its conduct and an effective aid to the congregation's participation therein. The order sought and achieved in worship, however, should be free from rigid formality. The worship should begin with praise to God and end with a benediction from Him.

The public worship of God should evidence due regard both for the historical forms and usages of the Church and the local traditions and usages of a congregation.

Public worship should be conducted according to an alternating principle whereby the scene may shift throughout the act of worship from Heaven to Earth and Earth to Heaven, from God to the worshiper and the worshiper to God: God acts and the worshiper responds; the worshiper acts and God responds.

The ends of public worship should always be the glory and reverence of God in Christ, the edification of the worshiper and the winning of souls to a corporate allegiance to Jesus Christ our Lord.

These ends demand not only order in the public worship of God, but a reverence for His House as evidenced in silence and proper decorum, the enrichment of the worship experience with

11

an intelligent — and intelligible on the part of the congregation —
use of Christian symbolism, meaningful and appropriate public
prayers, hymns and anthems, and wisely selected Scripture readings for doctrine, instruction and reproof. Not least of these
demands is the Minister's own personal and spiritual preparation
for leading his congregation in public worship. He is under holy
obligation not only to develop his powers for an effectual preaching of the Word of God, but for so guiding the experience of
corporate worship that it will satisfy the spiritual needs of the
congregation, express their holy desires, and become a meaningful
response to God's acts in the worship.

A MORNING WORSHIP SERVICE (1)

PRELUDE

CHORAL CALL TO WORSHIP

PROCESSIONAL HYMN

OPENING SENTENCES AND INVOCATION

DOXOLOGY

OLD TESTAMENT LESSON AND GLORIA PATRI

NEW TESTAMENT LESSON

PASTORAL PRAYER AND CHANT

ANTHEM

[ANNOUNCEMENTS]*

SILENT MEDITATION AND SERMON HYMN

SERMON AND BRIEF PRAYER

[INVITATION HYMN]

OFFERING, DEDICATION OF OFFERING, AND CHORAL RESPONSE

RECESSIONAL HYMN

BENEDICTION

POSTLUDE

*Items in brackets are optional.

The Congregation shall enter the Sanctuary in silence and engage briefly in silent prayer as a part of their preparation for the worship.

PRELUDE: *(An appreciative silence shall obtain while the Prelude is being played.)*

CHORAL CALL TO WORSHIP: *(Following the Prelude, the Choir, assembled at some point outside the Sanctuary, shall sing a Call to Worship, such as "The Lord is in His Holy Temple.")*

PROCESSIONAL HYMN: *(The Choir, joined by the standing Congregation, shall sing a Processional Hymn as they enter the Sanctuary.)*

OPENING SENTENCES: *(After the Processional Hymn, the Minister shall give the Opening Sentences and Invocation.)*

O Lord, open thou my lips; and my mouth shall show forth thy praise. For thou desirest not sacrifice; else would I give it: thou delightest not in burnt offering. The sacrifices of God are a broken spirit: a broken and a contrite heart, O God, thou wilt not despise. — Psalm 51:15-17.

— *or* —

O come, let us sing unto the Lord: let us make a joyful noise to the rock of our salvation. Let us come before his presence with thanksgiving, and make a joyful noise unto him with psalms. — Psalm 95:1-2.

— *or* —

Seek ye the Lord while he may be found, call ye upon him while he is near. — Isaiah 55:6.

— *or* —

God is a Spirit: and they that worship him must worship him in spirit and in truth. — John 4:24.

INVOCATION: *(This may be given in the following or similar words.)*

Almighty God, our heavenly Father, who art the God of all grace: Be Thou with us in our praise and prayer and in the preaching of Thy Word and teach us to worship Thee in spirit and in truth. Help us, O God, to call upon Thy name

aright that in this Thy House we may rejoice and be glad in
Thee; through Jesus Christ our Lord. Amen.

Doxology:

Old Testament Lesson: (*Then the Congregation shall sing the
Gloria Patri and be seated.*)

New Testament Lesson:

Pastoral Prayer and Chant: (*After the New Testament Lesson, the Minister shall offer a Pastoral Prayer in the following
manner, expressing the Congregation's attitude of thanksgiving,
their contrition, the assurance of pardon, their desires for themselves and supplications for the world.*)

Most merciful and gracious God, our heavenly Father: We thank
Thee that Thou art the fountain of all mercy and blessing.
Thou openest Thy hand to us and satisfiest the longing soul and
fillest the hungry soul with Thy goodness. For Thy gifts of grace,
for the benefits we have received at Thy hand, we give Thee
thanks. Thou hast preserved our souls in life, granted health
and prosperity to many of us, and hast kept Thy abode with
the sick and afflicted and with those who have suffered misfortune. For all Thy blessings known and unknown to us, we
bless Thy holy name.

O ever blessed God, who art nigh unto them that are of a
broken heart, and savest such as be of a contrite spirit: We confess our sins before Thee and acknowledge our human frailty.
We have not always been obedient to Thy Word; nor have we
willingly obeyed Thy will. We have complained when we
should have been thankful. We have not been as considerate
of each other as Thou wouldst have Thy children be. Forgive
us, O Lord God, all our sins, our errors, our failings, and grant
us to be restored in fellowship with Thee and each other. Remember, O Lord, Thy tender mercies, and Thy lovingkindness,
for they have been ever as of old.

O Thou who forgivest all our sins and redeemest our soul
from destruction: Grant us to trust in Thy mercy and Thy
heavenly assurance of pardon. We hope in Thy Word which
assures us that he who comes to Thee will in no wise be cast
out. Thou removest our transgressions from us as the east is

from the west and restoreth unto us the joy of Thy salvation; for which we honor Thy name.

Almighty God who hearest prayer: Bless Thy Church. Grant that through us the Gospel may be spread throughout the world and that Thy saving health may be known to the nations. Overrule through the sovereignty of Thy Spirit the kingdom of sin. Nerve Thy Church militant and grant us communion with the saints.

We pray for the peace and tranquility of our state and nation. Grant that those who hold positions of power, influence, and great responsibility may seek Thy guidance and rely upon Thy aid.

Bless our homes and our children. Guard them. Secure them, and prosper them.

Protect the homeless, and provide for the needy.

Support the aged, and care for the infirm.

Heal the sick, and be a comfort to them.

Sustain the sorrowing, and bring peace to the troubled.

Confirm those who are weak in the faith, and encourage those whose labors and patience are yet unrewarded.

Grant, O heavenly Father, that in all things we may be blessed according to our need; through Jesus Christ our Lord. Amen.

CHANT OF AFFIRMATION: (*After the Pastoral Prayer, the Congregation shall render a Chant of Affirmation such as "The Lord Is My Shepherd."*)

ANTHEM: (*or Hymn*)

[ANNOUNCEMENTS]: (*These should be limited to necessary items of information, or omitted altogether.*)

SILENT MEDITATION AND SERMON HYMN: (*The Congregation shall stand for the singing of this Hymn.*)

SERMON AND BRIEF PRAYER: (*The Minister shall conclude his sermon with a Brief Prayer in which he implores God to act upon the hearers — believers and unbelievers alike — through the Holy Spirit, so that the preached Word may accomplish in some measure its end.*)

[Invitation Hymn]: *(This may be sung at this point for the purpose of receiving new members into the Church.* The Congregation shall stand.)*

Offering: *(The Minister shall speak an Offertory Sentence before the Offering is collected. While the Offering is being collected by the Ushers or Deacons, a vocal solo, choral anthem, or organ selection may be given.)*

Offertory Sentences:
Every man shall give as he is able, according to the blessing of the Lord thy God which he hath given thee. — Deuteronomy 16:17.

— *or* —

What shall I render unto the Lord for all his benefits toward me? I will pay my vows unto the Lord now in the presence of all his people. — Psalm 116:12,14.

— *or* —

Upon the first day of the week let every one of you lay by him in store, as God hath prospered him. — I Corinthians 16:2.

Dedication of the Offering: *(The Offering having been collected and the Ushers or Deacons now standing before the pulpit, the Minister shall dedicate the Offering. The Congregation shall stand for this Dedication and remain standing until after the Choral Response.)*

Choral Response: *(The Dedication of the Offering shall be followed by an appropriate Choral Response, such as "All things come of Thee, O Lord, and of Thine own have we given Thee. Amen.")*

Recessional Hymn: *(The Choir shall now retire from the Sanctuary. The Congregation joins in the singing of this Hymn, and remains seated through the Benediction.)*

Benediction:
The Lord bless thee, and keep thee: the Lord make his face

---

*Optional. The Congregation may have in use another and more desirable procedure for receiving new members into its fellowship.

shine upon thee, and be gracious unto Thee: the Lord lift up his countenance upon thee, and give thee peace. Amen. — Numbers 6:24-26.

— or —

The grace of the Lord Jesus Christ, and the love of God, and the communion of the Holy Spirit, be with you all. Amen. — II Corinthians 13:14.

— or —

And the peace of God, which passeth all understanding, shall keep your hearts and minds through Christ Jesus. Amen. — Philippians 4:7.

A MORNING WORSHIP SERVICE (2)

PRELUDE

PROCESSIONAL HYMN

CALL TO WORSHIP

INVOCATION

HYMN OF PRAISE

RESPONSIVE READING FROM THE PSALTER

CHORAL CHANT

LESSON FROM THE OLD TESTAMENT

HYMN OF THE HOLY SPIRIT OR THE WORD OF GOD

LESSON FROM THE NEW TESTAMENT

PASTORAL PRAYER

HYMN OF TRUST OR ASSURANCE

[ANNOUNCEMENTS]*

OFFERING (*During this time an Offertory Solo or Anthem may be sung, or an Organ Selection played.*)

DEDICATION OF OFFERING

*Items in brackets are optional.

DOXOLOGY
SILENT PREPARATION FOR THE SERMON (*brief pause*)
SERMON HYMN
SERMON
BRIEF PRAYER
[INVITATION HYMN]
BENEDICTION
RECESSIONAL HYMN
POSTLUDE

A MORNING WORSHIP SERVICE (3)

PRELUDE
PROCESSIONAL HYMN
CALL TO WORSHIP
INVOCATION
HYMN OF PRAISE
PRAYER
RESPONSIVE READING FROM THE PSALTER
HYMN OF THE HOLY SPIRIT OR THE WORD OF GOD
LESSON FROM THE OLD TESTAMENT
HYMN OF ASPIRATION OR LOVE AND GRATITUDE, OR AN ANTHEM
LESSON FROM THE NEW TESTAMENT
PASTORAL PRAYER, FOLLOWED BY THE LORD'S PRAYER
[ANNOUNCEMENTS]*
SERMON HYMN
SERMON
PRAYER
[INVITATION HYMN]

*Items in brackets are optional.

OFFERING (*During this time an Offertory Solo or Anthem may be sung or an Organ Selection played.*)
DEDICATION OF OFFERING
DOXOLOGY
BENEDICTION
RECESSIONAL HYMN
POSTLUDE

AN EVENING WORSHIP SERVICE (1)

PRELUDE
[PROCESSIONAL HYMN]*
CALL TO WORSHIP AND INVOCATION
HYMN
LESSON FROM THE SCRIPTURES
PRAYER
MUSIC
DEVOTIONAL TALK OR BRIEF SERMON
SILENT MEDITATION
[INVITATION HYMN]
OFFERING AND DEDICATION OF OFFERING
[ANNOUNCEMENTS]
CLOSING HYMN OR RECESSIONAL HYMN
BENEDICTION
POSTLUDE

The Evening Worship Service is less formal and usually shorter than the Morning Worship Service. It may be meditative or evangelistic in character, depending upon the traditions and practices of the local congregation. The Evening Order described here is

*Items in brackets are optional.

meditative in character; it is followed by a suggestive outline of
an evangelistic order of service.

PRELUDE:

[PROCESSIONAL HYMN]

CALL TO WORSHIP:
It is a good thing to give thanks unto the Lord, and to sing
praises unto thy name, O most High: To show forth thy lovingkindness in the morning, and thy faithfulness every night. —
Psalm 92:1-2.

— *or* —

Remember thy congregation, which thou hast purchased of old;
the rod of thine inheritance, which thou hast redeemed; this
mount Zion, wherein thou hast dwelt.
    The day is thine, the night also is thine: thou hast prepared
the light and the sun.
    Thou hast set all the borders of the earth: thou hast made
summer and winter.
    Praise ye the Lord. Praise the Lord, O my soul. — Psalm
74:2, 16-17; 146:1.

INVOCATION (*in the following or similar words*)
Eternal God, our heavenly Father, who art enthroned above the
circle of the earth and orderest the day and the night to be a
blessing to Thy children: We turn to Thee at the close of this
day in our evening sacrifice of praise and prayer. Hallow these
moments in which, withdrawn from the tumult of life without,
we seek the rest of Thine own peace through the evening hours
and the inward power of Thy Spirit for the coming day; through
Jesus Christ our Lord. Amen.

HYMN: (*an evening hymn of praise*)

LESSON FROM THE SCRIPTURES:

PRAYER: (*in the following or similar words*)
Almighty God and Father of us all, we thank Thee that with
us Thy ways of love and mercy are known. Thou dost love us
with an everlasting love and dost restore us again and again to

favor with Thee through the wideness of Thy mercy. Yet we are prone toward unfaithfulness to Thee and vengefulness toward our fellow man while Thou art ever merciful toward us. Be pleased, O God, to grant unto us Thy pardoning grace that we may end this day in peace with Thee and in fellowship with the faithful.

Help us to love Thee as we ought, revealing in our lives — in what we think and do — the indwelling of the Holy Spirit. Fill us with compassion for each other that we may be worthy of being called followers of Thy compassionate Son, Jesus Christ, our Lord. Let the power of Thy Spirit descend upon us in this hour that, worshiping Thee in spirit and in truth, we may be saved from all coldness of heart and inhospitality of spirit. Let Thy name be honored as we lift up our hearts to Thee, O God, and bless each expectant worshiper with the light of Thy countenance; through Jesus Christ our Lord. Amen.

MUSIC: *(hymn of the Holy Spirit or an anthem)*

DEVOTIONAL TALK OR BRIEF SERMON:

SILENT MEDITATION AND COMMITMENT:

[INVITATION HYMN, *to receive new members*]

OFFERING: *(A musical selection may be played or sung.)*

DEDICATION OF OFFERING

[ANNOUNCEMENTS]

CLOSING HYMN: *(or Recessional Hymn)*

BENEDICTION:

The grace of the Lord Jesus Christ, and the love of God, and the communion of the Holy Spirit, be with you all. Amen. — II Corinthians 13:14.

— *or* —

Now unto the King eternal, immortal, invisible, the only wise God, be honour and glory for ever and ever. Amen. — I Timothy 1:17.

AN EVENING WORSHIP SERVICE (2)

CONGREGATIONAL SINGING OF FAMILIAR GOSPEL HYMNS

[PROCESSIONAL HYMN]*

CALL TO WORSHIP

HYMN *(an evening hymn of praise)*

INVOCATION

LESSON FROM THE SCRIPTURES

PRAYER

HYMN *(one or more gospel hymns)*

SERMON

PRAYER

INVITATION HYMN *(to receive new members)*

OFFERING *(During this time a musical selection may be played or sung)*

DEDICATION OF OFFERING

[ANNOUNCEMENTS]

CLOSING HYMN *(or the Recessional Hymn)*

BENEDICTION

*Items in brackets are optional.

Calls to Worship

GENERAL CALLS TO WORSHIP

Thus saith the Lord our God, Verily my sabbaths ye shall keep; for it is a sign between me and you throughout your generations; that ye may know that I am the Lord that doth sanctify you. — Exodus 31:13.

It is a good thing to give thanks unto the Lord, and to sing praises unto thy name, O most High: To shew forth thy lovingkindness in the morning, and thy faithfulness every night. — Psalm 92:1-2.

O come, let us worship and bow down: let us kneel before the Lord our maker. For he is our God; and we are the people of his pasture, and the sheep of his hand. — Psalm 95:6-7.

CALLS TO MORNING WORSHIP

My voice shalt thou hear in the morning, O Lord; in the morning will I direct my prayer unto thee, and will look up.—Psalm 5:3.

O God, thou art my God; early will I seek thee: my soul thirsteth for thee; my flesh longeth for thee in a dry and thirsty land where no water is; To see thy power and thy glory, so as I have seen thee in the sanctuary. — Psalm 63:1-2.

CALLS TO EVENING WORSHIP

Blessed be the name of the Lord from this time forth and for evermore. From the rising of the sun unto the going down of the same the Lord's name is to be praised. — Psalm 113:2-3.

Behold, bless ye the Lord, all ye servants of the Lord, which by night stand in the house of the Lord. Lift up your hands in the sanctuary, and bless the Lord. — Psalm 134:1-2.

CALLS TO COMMUNION OR EASTER WORSHIP

Thus saith the Lord our God, This day shall be unto you as a memorial; and ye shall keep it a feast to the Lord throughout your generations; ye shall keep it a feast by an ordinance forever. — Exodus 12:14.

And we declare unto you glad tidings, how that the promise which was made unto the fathers, God hath fulfilled the same unto us their children, in that he hath raised up Jesus again. — Acts 13:32-33.

Christ our passover is sanctified for us: Therefore let us keep the feast. — I Corinthians 5:7b-8a.

CALLS TO PENITENCE AND SPIRITUAL RENEWAL

The Lord is nigh unto all them that call upon him, to all that call upon him in truth. He will fulfill the desire of them that fear him: he also will hear their cry, and will save them — Psalm 145: 18-19.

Seek ye the Lord while he may be found, call ye upon him while he is near: Let the wicked forsake his way, and the unrighteous man his thoughts: and let him return unto the Lord, and he will have mercy upon him; and to our God, for he will abundantly pardon. — Isaiah 55:6-7.

CALLS TO GOOD FRIDAY WORSHIP

All we like sheep have gone astray; we have turned everyone to his own way; and the Lord hath laid on him the iniquity of us all. — Isaiah 53:6.

The Son of man must suffer many things, and be rejected of the elders and chief priests and scribes, and be slain, and be raised the third day. Let these sayings sink down into your ears for the Son of man shall be delivered into the hands of men. — Luke 9:22, 44.

CALLS TO PALM SUNDAY WORSHIP

Lift up your heads, O ye gates; even lift them up, ye everlasting doors; and the King of glory shall come in. Who is this King of glory? The Lord of hosts, he is the King of glory. — Psalm 24:9-10.

Blessed be the King that cometh in the name of the Lord: peace in heaven, and glory in the highest. — Luke 19:38.

CALLS TO THANKSGIVING DAY WORSHIP

Give unto the Lord the glory due unto his name; bring an offering, and come before him: worship the Lord in the beauty of holiness. — I Chronicles 16:29.

O bless our God, ye people, and make the voice of his praise to be heard; which holdeth our soul in life, and suffereth not our feet to be moved. Come and hear, all ye that fear God, and I will declare what he hath done for my soul. — Psalm 66:8-9, 16.

Rejoice evermore. In everything give thanks: for this is the will of God in Christ Jesus concerning you. — I Thessalonians 5:16, 18.

CALLS TO CHRISTMAS DAY WORSHIP

The Lord hath said unto me, Thou art my Son; this day have I begotten thee. — Psalm 2:7b.

Behold, the tabernacle of God is with men, and he will dwell with them, and they shall be his people, and God himself shall be with them, and be their God. — Revelation 21:3.

CALLS TO WATCH NIGHT WORSHIP

Thy years, O God, are throughout all generations. Thou art the same, and thy years shall have no end. — Psalm 102:24, 27.

The mercy of the Lord is from everlasting to everlasting upon them that fear him, and his righteousness unto children's children; To such as keep his covenant, and to those that remember his commandments to do them. The Lord hath prepared his throne in the heavens; and his Kingdom ruleth over all. — Psalm 103:17-19.

CALLS TO NEW YEAR'S DAY WORSHIP

In God is my salvation and my glory: the rock of my strength, and my refuge, is in God. Trust in him at all times; ye people, pour out your heart before him: God is a refuge for us. — Psalm 61:7-8.

I am Alpha and Omega, the beginning and the end, the first and the last. — Revelation 22:13.

Prayers of Invocation

FROM THE BIBLE*

My God, let, I beseech thee, thine eyes be open, and let thine ears be attent unto the prayer that is made in this place. — II Chronicles 6:40.

O send out thy light and thy truth: let them lead me; let them bring me unto thy holy hill, and to thy tabernacles. Then will I go unto the altar of God, unto God my exceeding joy: yea, upon the harp will I praise thee, O God my God. — Psalm 43:3-4.

Praise waiteth for thee, O God, in Zion: and unto thee shall the vow be performed. O thou that hearest prayer, unto thee shall all flesh come. — Psalm 65:1-2.

My prayer is unto thee, O Lord, in an acceptable time: O God, in the multitude of thy mercy hear me, in the truth of thy salvation. — Psalm 69:13.

*Prayers of Invocation from the Bible may be concluded with an Amen.

Let all those that seek thee rejoice and be glad in thee: and let such as love thy salvation say continually, Let God be magnified. — Psalm 70:4.

Open to me the gates of righteousness: I will go into them, and I will praise the Lord: This gate of the Lord, into which the righteous shall enter. I will praise thee: for thou hast heard me, and art become my salvation. — Psalm 118:19-21.

I stretch forth my hands unto thee: my soul thirsteth after thee, as a thirsty land. Cause me to hear thy loving-kindness in the morning; for in thee do I trust: cause me to know the way wherein I should walk; for I lift up my soul unto thee. — Psalm 143:6, 8.

FROM OTHER SOURCES

Almighty God, unto whom all hearts are open, all desires known, and from whom no secrets are hid; cleanse the thoughts of our hearts by the inspiration of thy Holy Spirit, that we may perfectly love thee, and worthily magnify thy holy name; through Christ our Lord. Amen. — Gregorian Sacramentary, 7th Century.

Almighty God, who hast given us grace at this time with one accord to make our common supplications unto thee; and dost promise that when two or three are gathered together in thy Name thou wilt grant their requests; Fulfil now, O Lord, the desires and petitions of thy servants, as may be most expedient for them; granting us in this world knowledge of thy truth, and in the world to come life everlasting. Amen. — A Prayer of St. Chrysostom.

O God, the preparation of the heart and the opening of the lips are from Thee. Quicken us after Thy lovingkindness, that we may call aright upon Thy name. Meet with us in prayer and praise and in the Word. Make this a day of grace and blessing to us all in Thy House, for Jesus' sake. Amen. — A New Directory for the Public Worship of God.

Offertory Sentences and Prayers

BEFORE THE OFFERING

Thus saith the Lord our God: Of every man that giveth it willingly with his heart ye shall take my offering. — Exodus 25:2b.

This is the thing which the Lord commanded, saying, Take ye from among you an offering unto the Lord: Whosoever is of a willing heart, let him bring it, an offering of the Lord. — Exodus 35:4b-5.

Every man shall give as he is able, according to the blessing of the Lord thy God which he hath given thee. — Deuteronomy 16:17.

What shall I render unto the Lord for all his benefits toward me? I will pay my vows unto the Lord now in the presence of all his people. — Psalm 116:12, 14.

Hear the words of our Lord Jesus Christ: Freely ye have received, freely give. — Matthew 10:8b.

Every man according as he purposeth in his heart, so let him give; not grudgingly, or of necessity: For God loveth a cheerful giver. And God is able to make all grace abound toward you; that ye, always having all sufficiency in all things, may abound to every good work. — I Corinthians 9:7-8.

AFTER THE OFFERING

All things come of thee, O Lord, and of thine own have we given thee. — I Chronicles 29:14.

Blessed be the Lord, who daily loadeth us with benefits, even the God of our salvation. — Psalm 68:19.

The eyes of all wait upon thee; and thou givest them their meat in due season. Thou openest thine hand, and satisfiest the desire of every living thing. The Lord is righteous in all his ways, and holy in all his works. — Psalm 145:15-17.

Benedictions

APOSTOLIC

The grace of the Lord Jesus Christ, and the love of God, and the communion of the Holy Ghost, be with you all. Amen. — I Corinthians 13:14.

PRIESTLY

The Lord bless thee, and keep thee:

The Lord make his face shine upon thee, and be gracious unto thee:

The Lord lift up his countenance upon thee, and give thee peace. Amen. — Numbers 6:24-26.

THE COMMUNION SERVICE

Now the God of peace, that brought again from the dead our Lord Jesus, that great shepherd of the sheep, through the blood of the everlasting covenant, make you perfect in every good work to do his will, working in you that which is well pleasing in his sight, through Jesus Christ; to whom be glory forever and ever. Amen. — Hebrews 13:20-21.

THE FUNERAL SERVICE

Now unto him that is able to keep you from falling, and to present you faultless before the presence of his glory with exceeding joy, To the only wise God our Saviour, be glory and majesty, dominion and power, both now and ever. Amen. — Jude 24-25.

THE CHURCH ANNIVERSARY
(OR RELIGIOUS CONVOCATION)

Now unto him that is able to do exceeding abundantly above all that we ask or think, according to the power that worketh in us,

Unto him be glory in the church by Christ Jesus throughout all ages, world without end. Amen. — Ephesians 3:20-21.

THE GENERAL SERVICE

God be merciful unto us, and bless us; and cause his face to shine upon us; That thy way may be known upon earth, thy saving health among all nations. Amen. — Psalm 67:1-2.

Now unto the King eternal, immortal, invisible, the only wise God, be honour and glory forever and ever. Amen. — I Timothy 1:17.

SECTION TWO

The Administration of the Ordinances (Sacraments)

GUIDING PRINCIPLES AND PRACTICAL SUGGESTIONS

The Ordinances of the Church are commands of our Lord Jesus Christ to His Church. They, therefore, concern the whole congregation and should be administered in the presence of the congregation, as far as this is possible.

Participation in the observance of these Ordinances is a duty and a privilege of every believer. They are observed not only as an act of obedience to God in Christ but as a means of grace to all who share in these rites.

The Administration of the Ordinances is the Holy Word dramatized — God's Word in action. As we see this spiritual drama, we remember the sacrificial and redeeming love of God through His Son Jesus Christ. We participate in this administration as committed believers in the efficacy of God's grace through repentance, faith and obedience. We observe the Ordinances as the people of His purchase, as His workmanship, and as the partakers of His life and strength.

The Minister should see to it that new converts are duly instructed in the faith to which they are now committed and which they have professed publicly. They should be taught the privileges and responsibilities of Church membership, and the meaning of the Church Ordinances. A number of special class sessions, adequate to cover the subjects proposed, should be arranged by the Minister for the new converts.

The Minister should also see to it that the whole Congregation is duly instructed in the meaning of the faith. They should be inspired and guided into a daily and consistent appropriation of the means of grace, and impressed with their duty to observe through their daily lives what the Ordinances of the Church symbolize.

31

Special sermons, lectures, and discussions directed to these ends should issue in encouraging results.

Preparation of the Congregation for the administration of the Ordinances of the Church, especially the celebration of The Lord's Supper, should be encouraged by the Minister. A time should be set for this preparation of the Congregation and of himself prior to the actual celebration of the rite.

Local traditions and usages of the Congregation should not be disregarded by the Minister; yet he should at all times be diligent, prayerful and patient in guiding his people to what is most acceptable to God, as he understands His will through the Scriptures, and to what is most meaningful and edifying to them as he, their shepherd, is given the knowledge and the wisdom by the Holy Spirit to perceive this.

BAPTISM SERVICE

OPENING SENTENCES AND INVOCATION

HYMN

SCRIPTURES

PRAYER

HYMN

BAPTISM

SERMON OR ADDRESS

HYMN

OFFERING AND DEDICATION

BENEDICTION

The Candidates for Baptism should be dressed and ready for Baptism at the hour appointed for this Service. They should be seated on the front pew (or pews) when the Service begins. It is suggested that an Assistant or Associate Minister preside over the first part of this Service so that the Minister may have time to make his own preparations for the Baptism.

Prior to entering the Sanctuary, the Candidates, when they are dressed, should be assembled in some convenient room so that the

Minister may explain to them his Baptismal Procedure: What questions shall be put to them by the Minister before they are baptized; what they are to answer; how they are to hold their hands and conduct themselves in the Baptistery; and how he will proceed with the actual baptizing.

All of this should be done early enough so that the Candidates may be in their seats in the Sanctuary in time for the beginning of the Service. When the hour arrives for the beginning of the Service, the Minister in charge shall enter the Sanctuary and, from the pulpit, shall say one or more Sentences from Holy Scripture and shall give the Invocation. The Congregation shall stand through the singing of the first Hymn.

OPENING SENTENCES:

It is a good thing to give thanks unto the Lord, and to sing praises unto thy name, O Most High:

To show forth thy lovingkindness in the morning, and thy faithfulness every night,

For thou, Lord, hast made me glad through thy work: I will triumph in the works of thy hands.

O Lord, how great are thy works! and thy thoughts are very deep. — Psalm 92:1-2, 4-5.

INVOCATION: *(in the following or similar words)*

O Lord God, our heavenly Father: Open Thou our lips and our mouths shall show forth Thy praise. Quicken our hearts by the outpouring of the Holy Spirit that we may worship Thee in spirit and in truth. Satisfy us with the goodness of Thy House and be known to us in the administration of the Ordinance of Baptism, which Thou Thyself hast commanded us to observe; through Jesus Christ our Lord. Amen.

HYMN: *(a hymn of praise, such as one of the following)*

"O for a Heart to Praise My God"

"O for a Thousand Tongues to Sing"

"Come, Thou Fount of Every Blessing"

"My God, the Spring of All My Joys"

SCRIPTURE:

Go ye therefore, and teach all nations, baptizing them in the name of the Father, and of the Son, and of the Holy Ghost:

Teaching them to observe all things whatsoever I have commanded you: and, lo, I am with you always, even unto the end of the world. Amen. — Matthew 28:19-20.

— or —

John did baptize in the wilderness, and preach the baptism of repentance for the remission of sins.

And preached, saying, There cometh one mightier than I after me, the latchet of whose shoes I am not worthy to stoop down and unloose.

I indeed have baptized you with water: but he shall baptize you with the Holy Ghost. — Mark 1:4, 7-8.

— or —

Know ye not, that so many of us as were baptized into Jesus Christ were baptized into his death?

Therefore we are buried with him by baptism into death: that like as Christ was raised up from the dead by the glory of the Father, even so we also should walk in newness of life. — Romans 6:3-4.

— or —

For ye are all the children of God by faith in Christ Jesus.

For as many of you as have been baptized into Christ have put on Christ. — Galatians 3:26-27.

PRAYER: *(in the following or similar words)*
Almighty and gracious God, who in Thy love didst sacrifice Thy Son for our sakes: We thank Thee that Thou hast made us partakers of Thy great mercy and the fellowship of Thy love. By Thy grace we have been brought into the fellowship of faith through membership in the Church. As Thou hast appointed the Ordinance of Baptism for those who believe on Thy Son, to be administered by the Church, grant, we beseech Thee, Thy Holy Spirit to approve and seal this act with His power. May these Candidates, who are to receive the baptism of water, be granted the baptism of the Spirit and of fire that they may live and serve Thee worthily and be preserved blameless for entrance into Thy heavenly Kingdom; through Jesus Christ our Lord. Amen.

HYMN: (*a hymn of the provisions of the Gospel, such as one of the following, the congregation standing*)

"Amazing Grace, How Sweet the Sound"

"How Sweet the Name of Jesus Sounds"

"I've Found a Friend, O Such a Friend"

"I Hear the Saviour Say"

"O Happy Day That Fixed My Choice"

BAPTISM: (*The Minister shall now proceed with the Baptism of Candidates. He shall want to address a few words to the Congregation before the Baptism begins. Then one by one he shall receive the Candidates into the Baptistery, instructing each to fold his arms across his breast. He shall then ask each Candidate in turn the following questions, which each must answer in the affirmative.*)

The Minister:

Do you believe on the Lord Jesus Christ?

The Candidate:

I do.

The Minister:

In obedience to the great command of the Head of the Church, and upon the profession of your faith, my *Brother*, I now baptize you in the name of the Father, and of the Son, and of the Holy Spirit.

The Minister shall then direct the Candidate to hold his breath and to be perfectly relaxed as he is gently lowered into the water. Burying all of the Candidate's body, the Minister shall then bring him gently up out of the water. In the case of an exceptionally tall Candidate, the Minister shall direct him to bend his knees, as though stooping, in order to protect his immersion from any hazard. It will not be necessary in any case for the Minister to throw the Candidate into the water with such force as to cause a great splash.

After the Candidates have been baptized, they shall go immediately to their dressing room and prepare to return to their seats in the Sanctuary.

The Minister shall prepare himself for returning to the Sanctuary and the Pulpit.

> During the entire Administration of Baptism, the Choir shall lead the congregation in singing softly appropriate and familiar hymns.

Sermon or Address: (*While the Candidates and the Minister are preparing to return to the Sanctuary, a Brief Sermon or Address may be delivered to the Congregation on some subject dealing with Evangelical Christianity and the Congregation's responsibility to the new member*).

Hymn: (*on the provisions of the Gospel, the congregation standing*)

Offering and Dedication:

Benediction:

The grace of the Lord Jesus Christ, and the love of God, and the communion of the Holy Spirit, be with you all. Amen.

LORD'S SUPPER SERVICE

Opening Sentences and Invocation

Hymn

Ten Commandments and Summary

Hymn

The Beatitudes

The Epistle

Hymn

Table Talk*

Sermon*

Offering and Dedication

Prayer of Thanksgiving and Consecration

The Lord's Supper

Hymn

Benediction

> This Service may be a part of the regular Morning or Evening

*If a table talk is planned, a Sermon should be omitted, or vice-versa.

*Order of Worship, but, when so used, the necessary alterations
should be made. This Order assumes that this will be a separate
Service.*

*When all necessary preparations have been made for this Serv-
ice, at the appointed hour the Minister shall enter the Sanctuary
to begin the observance with the following or similar Opening
Sentences from Holy Scripture. The Congregation shall stand
through the singing of the first Hymn.*

OPENING SENTENCES:

O give thanks unto the Lord, for he is good: for his mercy
endureth for ever.

Oh that men would praise the Lord for his goodness, and for
his wonderful works to the children of men! — Psalm 107:1, 8.

Who shall ascend into the hill of the Lord? or who shall stand
in his holy place? He that hath clean hands, and a pure heart;
who hath not lifted up his soul unto vanity, nor sworn deceitfully. — Psalm 24:3-4.

INVOCATION: *(in the following or similar words)*

We bless Thy glorious name, O God, for the gift of Thy Son for
the redemption of the world, and for the changes Thou, through
the Holy Spirit, hast wrought in our heart. Grant us Thy grace
now that, as we worship Thy Holy Name, we may do so with a
true heart and a humble and contrite spirit. May what we do in
this Service meet with Thine approval that Thou mayest be
known to us in the breaking of bread; through Jesus Christ our
Lord. Amen.

HYMN:

"O for a Heart to Praise, My God"
"According to Thy Gracious Word"
"Amazing Grace, How Sweet the Sound"
"Jesus, Thou Joy of Loving Hearts"

THE TEN COMMANDMENTS AND SUMMARY OF THE LAW:

And God spake all these words, saying,
I am the Lord thy God, which have brought thee out of the
land of Egypt, out of the house of bondage.
Thou shalt have no other gods before me.

Thou shalt not make unto thee any graven image, or any likeness of any thing that is in heaven above, or that is in the earth beneath, or that is in the water under the earth:

Thou shalt not bow down thyself to them, nor serve them: for I the Lord thy God am a jealous God, visiting the iniquity of the fathers upon the children unto the third and fourth generation of them that hate me;

And showing mercy unto thousands of them that love me, and keep my commandments.

Thou shalt not take the name of the Lord thy God in vain; for the Lord will not hold him guiltless that taketh his name in vain.

Remember the sabbath day, to keep it holy.

Six days shalt thou labor, and do all thy work:

But the seventh day is the sabbath of the Lord thy God: in it thou shalt not do any work, thou, nor thy son, nor thy daughter, thy manservant, nor thy maidservant, nor thy cattle, nor thy stranger that is within thy gates:

For in six days the Lord made heaven and earth, the sea, and all that in them is, and rested the seventh day: wherefore the Lord blessed the sabbath day, and hallowed it.

Honour thy father and thy mother: that thy days may be long upon the land which the Lord thy God giveth thee.

Thou shalt not kill.

Thou shalt not commit adultery.

Thou shalt not steal.

Thou shalt not bear false witness against thy neighbour.

Thou shalt not covet thy neighbour's house, thou shalt not covet thy neighbour's wife, nor his manservant, nor his maidservant, nor his ox, nor his ass, nor any thing that is thy neighbour's. — Exodus 20:1-17.

Hear the Summary of these Commandments in the words of Jesus Christ our Lord:

Thou shalt love the Lord thy God with all thy heart, and with all thy soul, and with all thy mind. This is the first and great commandment.

And the second is like unto it, Thou shalt love thy neighbour as thyself. — Matthew 22:37-39.

Hymn: *(the congregation standing)*
   "Break Thou the Bread of Life"
   "Shepherd of Souls, Refresh and Bless"
   "In the Cross of Christ I Glory"
   " 'Tis Midnight and on Olive's Brow"

The Beatitudes:

And seeing the multitudes, he went up into a mountain: and when he was set, his disciples came unto him:

And he opened his mouth, and taught them, saying,

Blessed are the poor in spirit: for theirs is the kingdom of heaven.

Blessed are they that mourn: for they shall be comforted.

Blessed are the meek: for they shall inherit the earth.

Blessed are they which do hunger and thirst after righteousness: for they shall be filled.

Blessed are the merciful: for they shall obtain mercy.

Blessed are the pure in heart: for they shall see God.

Blessed are the peacemakers: for they shall be called the children of God.

Blessed are they which are persecuted for righteousness' sake: for theirs is the kingdom of heaven.

Blessed are ye, when men shall revile you, and persecute you, and shall say all manner of evil against you falsely, for my sake.

Rejoice, and be exceeding glad: for great is your reward in heaven: for so persecuted they the prophets which were before you.

Ye are the salt of the earth: but if the salt have lost his savour, wherewith shall it be salted? It is thenceforth good for nothing, but to be cast out, and to be trodden under foot of men.

Ye are the light of the world. A city that is set on a hill cannot be hid.

Neither do men light a candle, and put it under a bushel, but on a candlestick; and it giveth light unto all that are in the house.

Let your light so shine before men, that they may see your

good works, and glorify your Father which is in heaven. — Matthew 5:1-16.

THE EPISTLES:

For I have received of the Lord that which also I delivered unto you, That the Lord Jesus the same night in which he was betrayed took bread:

And when he had given thanks, he brake it, and said, Take, eat: this is my body, which is broken for you: this do in remembrance of me.

After the same manner also he took the cup, when he had supped, saying, This cup is the new testament in my blood: this do ye, as oft as ye drink it, in remembrance of me.

For as often as ye eat this bread, and drink this cup, ye do show the Lord's death till he come.

Wherefore whosoever shall eat this bread, and drink this cup of the Lord, unworthily, shall be guilty of the body and blood of the Lord.

But let a man examine himself, and so let him eat of that bread, and drink of that cup. — I Corinthians 11:23-28.

— or —

Now the works of the flesh are manifest, which are these; Adultery, fornication, uncleanness, lasciviousness.

Idolatry, witchcraft, hatred, variance, emulations, wrath, strife, seditions, heresies.

Envyings, murders, drunkenness, revellings, and such like: of the which I tell you before, as I have also told you in time past, that they which do such things shall not inherit the kingdom of God.

But the fruit of the Spirit is love, joy, peace, longsuffering, gentleness, goodness, faith,

Meekness, temperance: against such there is no law. — Galatians 5:19-23.

HYMN: (the congregation standing)

"I Gave My Life for Thee"
"The Old Rugged Cross"
"A Holy Air Is Breathing Round"

"Here at Thy Table, Lord"
"When I Survey the Wondrous Cross"

After this Hymn, the SERMON, OFFERING *and* DEDICATION OF
OFFERING *may follow; or, omitting the Sermon, following the
offering and its Dedication, the Minister may take his place behind
the Holy Table and from this point give a short* TABLE TALK.
Then the Minister shall offer a PRAYER OF THANKSGIVING AND
CONSECRATION.

PRAYER OF THANKSGIVING AND CONSECRATION: *(in the following
or similar words)*

Our gracious heavenly Father, The Father of our Lord and
Saviour Jesus Christ: We praise and bless Thee for all Thy gifts
and benefits towards us. We thank Thee for the Gospel that is
preached to us, for every means of grace, and the fellowship of
the saints on earth and in heaven, in which it is our privilege
to share. We thank Thee for Thy Church, but most of all we
thank Thee for Thy unspeakable gifts to us: grace and salvation through Thy Son. Give us a heart, O God, to praise Thee
worthily — a heart made worthy, by the power of Thy Holy
Spirit, to eat at Thy Table.

Forgive us our sins, O Lord, and lead us to forgive each
other our trespasses. Bind us all in one fellowship of love, and
may we draw nigh to Thee as Thou drawest nigh to us.

Be pleased, O gracious heavenly Father, to sanctify these
elements of bread and wine and so bless this Thine Ordinance
that we, in faith and love and obedience, may be spiritually
nourished and our souls preserved blameless unto the Lord's
Second Coming; through Jesus Christ our Lord. Amen.

THE LORD'S SUPPER: *(With the Deacons or Assistants standing before him, the Minister shall direct the distribution of the elements, using the following words.)*

THE BREAD

The Lord Jesus, the same night in which He was betrayed,
took bread, as I now do ministering in His name *(takes the
Bread)*: and when He had given thanks He brake it, and said,
Take, eat; this is My Body which is broken for you: this do in

remembrance of Me. (*The Minister hands Bread to Deacons or Assistants, who distribute it to the Congregation.*)

When the Bread has been distributed among the Deacons or Assistants, who will in turn distribute it among the Congregation, the Minister shall turn to the Wine.

THE WINE

After the same manner also He took the cup, as I now do ministering in His Name (*takes the Wine*), when He had supped, saying, This cup is the new covenant in My Blood: this do, as oft as ye drink it, in remembrance of Me. (*The Minister hands the Wine to Deacons or Assistants, who distribute it to the Congregation.*)

During the distribution of the Bread and Wine, the Congregation should be led by the Choir in singing very softly familiar and appropriate hymns; or soft organ music may be played. After the Congregation has been served, the Deacons or Assistants return to the Holy Table and the Minister serves them, and himself last. Then the Minister shall say:

TO THE CONGREGATION

For as often as ye eat this bread and drink this cup, ye do show the Lord's death till He come. Let us all now commune *together* in remembrance of Him.

After a moment of silence, the Communion glasses are collected or placed in holders at back of pews, the Holy Table re-covered and the members of the Congregation shake hands with those nearest to them, while a closing HYMN is being sung. Then shall the Minister give the BENEDICTION.

THE BENEDICTION:

Now the God of peace, that brought again from the dead our Lord Jesus, that great shepherd of the sheep, through the blood of the everlasting covenant, Make you perfect in every good work to do his will, working in you that which is wellpleasing in his sight, through Jesus Christ; to whom be glory forever and ever. Amen. — Hebrews 13:20-21.

SECTION THREE

Marriage and the Christian Family

GUIDING PRINCIPLES AND PRACTICAL SUGGESTIONS

Marriage is the foundation of the home and of all human fellowship. It is ordained of God and divinely established as the only approved way of replenishing the earth.

The Christian family is established for the mutual love and edification of the Christian husband and the Christian wife, the propagation and nurture of a Christian generation.

Christian family living is a duty as well as a privilege. It has its hard demands as well as its pleasures. Duty is to be the tie that binds when conjugal love needs repair. Mutual respect must always attend it, and daily personal concern and consideration direct it. Every effort, human and divine, should be employed to preserve it.

The Church can encourage and strengthen Christian family ties by emphasizing the divine approval of Christian marriage, the practical importance of the wedlock of Christian mates, and by forbidding all but Christian practices in the solemnization of marriage as a Christian rite. Due regard for family unity, encouragement, and convenience should be evidenced in the planning of the church's total program and in its provisions for Christian youth.

The Minister should achieve competence in counseling with Christian young people who have reached the courting age, with engaged couples, and with those whose marriage is in trouble. His counseling should, when necessary, lead to a referral of couples to the proper agency which is more competent and equipped than he to handle more than the ordinary pre-marital and marital problems.

The Minister's message at appropriate times on Christian Marriage and Family Living; his encouragement of young parents to dedicate their newborn babies to God through a proper and public rite; his suggestion that new home owners in the Congregation

43

dedicate their new homes to God through an appropriate service
in their homes — are all important and necessary contributions he
can make toward a more effectual ministry to Christian families.

MARRIAGE SERVICE

SPECIAL MUSIC
INTRODUCTION TO MARRIAGE CEREMONY
PRAYER
SCRIPTURE READING
MINISTERIAL CHARGE
MARRIAGE VOWS
THE RING SERVICE
DECLARATION OF MARRIAGE
PRAYER
THE LORD'S PRAYER
BLESSING
SPECIAL MUSIC:

*Following appropriate vocal selections by the choir or a soloist,
when the marriage is solemnized in a Church, the persons to be
married shall present themselves before the Minister, the Man at
the right hand of the Woman.*

INTRODUCTION TO MARRIAGE CEREMONY
Dearly beloved, we are gathered together here in the sight of
God and in the presence of this company, to join together this
man and this woman in holy matrimony. Marriage is an honorable estate, instituted of God, blessed by our Lord Jesus Christ,
and declared by Saint Paul to be honorable among all men. It is
not, therefore, to be entered into unadvisedly or lightly, but rev-
erently, soberly, advisedly, and in the fear of God. Let us, therefore, under the seriousness of this act, invoke the Divine
Presence upon this occasion.

PRAYER:
Almighty and gracious God, our heavenly Father, who settest
the solitary in families: Look in favor, we beseech Thee, upon

these Thy servants, this Man and this Woman. Be Thou the honored guest at their wedding and help them to speak the vows which they are about to make in sincerity and truth. Grant that they have been brought together by Thy Providence so that they may be truly and eternally joined together by Thy Holy Spirit; we pray through Jesus Christ our Lord. Amen.

Scripture Reading:

When solemnized in a Church, the Minister may read Psalm 128, introducing it with the following or similar words:

Hear the words of Holy Scripture concerning those who fear God as recorded in Psalm 128:

Blessed is every one that feareth the Lord; that walketh in his ways. For thou shalt eat the labour of thine hands: happy shalt thou be, and it shall be well with thee. Thy wife shall be as a fruitful vine by the sides of thine house: thy children like olive plants round about thy table. Behold, that thus shall the man be blessed that feareth the Lord. The Lord shall bless thee out of Zion: and thou shalt see the good of Jerusalem all the days of thy life. Yea, thou shalt see thy children's children, and peace upon Israel.

Then may the Minister conclude this Psalm with the following or similar words:

May this blessing be granted unto you.

Ministerial Charge:

I now charge you both, as you stand in the presence of God, to remember that true love and the faithful observance of your marriage vows are required as the foundation of a successful marriage and the establishment of a happy and enduring home. Without these there can be no real marriage and the home which you will endeavor to establish will be a vain effort. Keep the solemn vows you are about to make. Live with tender consideration for each other. Conduct your lives in honesty and in truth. And your marriage will last. Your home will endure. The marriage bond will be a blessing to you, and you will be a blessing to others. This should be remembered as you now declare your desire to be wed.

MARRIAGE VOWS

The Minister: (to the Man)
N., Do you take this woman to be your wedded wife? And do you solemnly promise, before God and these witnesses, that you will love her, comfort her, honor and keep her in sickness and in health; and that, forsaking all others for her alone, you will perform unto her all the duties that a husband owes to his wife, until God, by death, shall separate you?

The Man:
I do.

The Minister: (to the Woman)
N., Do you take this man to be your wedded husband? And do you solemnly promise, before God and these witnesses, that you will love him, comfort him, honor and keep him in sickness and in health; and that, forsaking all others for him alone, you will perform unto him all the duties that a wife owes to her husband, until God, by death, shall separate you?

The Woman:
I do.

The Minister: (to the Giver, when the Woman is given away)
Who giveth this Woman to be married to this Man?

The Giver:
I do. *(The Giver then retires to his seat.)*

The Minister: (to the Man and the Woman)
Since it is your desire to take each other as husband and wife, please join your right hands, and repeat after me, before God and these witnesses, the marriage vow.

The Man:
I, N., take thee, N., to be my wedded wife, to have and to hold from this day forward, for better or for worse, for richer or for poorer, in sickness and in health, to love and to cherish, till death us do part, according to God's holy ordinance; and, thereto, I plight thee my faith.

The Woman:

I, N., take thee, N., to be my wedded husband, to have and to hold from this day forward, for better or for worse, for richer or for poorer, in sickness and in health, to love and to cherish, till death us do part, according to God's holy ordinance; and, thereto, I plight thee my faith.

The Ring Service

The Man and the Woman shall loose hands. The Minister shall receive from the Man a ring, and, in the case of a double-ring ceremony, one also from the Woman.

The Minister: (holding up the ring or rings)

The wedding ring is an outward and visible sign of an inward and spiritual bond which unites two loyal hearts in endless love.

When two rings are used, the Minister shall ask the Woman and the Man in turn:

N., will you receive this ring from N., as a token of *his* affection, sincerity and fidelity toward you, and will you wear it as a symbol of your own affection, sincerity and fidelity toward *him?*

Each shall answer in turn: I will.

The Minister shall then give the Woman's ring to the Man to place on the fourth finger of her left hand. Then shall the Man say (or if two rings are used, the Woman shall receive from the Minister the Man's ring and say in turn):

The Man: (and Woman, when applicable)

This ring I give thee, in token and pledge of our constant faith and abiding love; with this ring I thee wed, and with all my earthy goods I thee endow.

Declaration of Marriage

The Minister: (to the Man and Woman)

Please join your right hands.

The Minister: (to the People)

For as much as N. and N. have consented together in holy wedlock and have witnessed the same before God and this company and thereto have given and pledged their faith, each to the other, and have declared the same by joining their right hands and by giving and receiving a ring, I declare, by the authority committed unto me as a Minister of the Gospel, that they are Husband and Wife, according to the ordinance of God and the law of this State, in the Name of the Father, and of the Son, and of the Holy Spirit. Amen.

The Husband and Wife kneel and remain kneeling through the blessing.

The Minister:

Those whom God hath joined together, let not man put asunder.

PRAYER:

O gracious and merciful God, our heavenly Father, of whom the whole family in heaven and earth is named: Be Thou pleased to seal the vows which these Thy servants have taken with Thine approval, and grant to this Husband and Wife all spiritual grace and the willingness to keep the vow and covenant between them made. Defend them amidst all temptation and save them from indifference and a love grown cold. In the midst of adversity or discord in their home be Thou their stay, O heavenly Father; and lighten their burdens by strengthening their spirits. May they live each for the other in peace and with a growing true affection that their home may be a haven of rest and a place of Thy abode; through Jesus Christ our Lord. Amen.

THE LORD'S PRAYER: *(When solemnized in a Church, here the Lord's Prayer may be sung by the choir or the soloist or said in unison by all the people.)*

THE BLESSING:

The Lord bless you and keep you: The Lord make his face shine upon you and be gracious unto you: The Lord lift up his countenance upon you and give you peace, both now and for evermore. Amen.

Then shall the Minister direct the Husband and Wife to rise. The Husband, lifting his Wife's veil, shall kiss her, thus concluding the ceremony.

SERVICE FOR THE RENEWAL OF MARRIAGE VOWS

OPENING SENTENCES
PRAYER
INTRODUCTION TO CEREMONY
PRAYER
RENEWAL OF VOWS
PRAYER FOR THE COUPLE
PRAYER FOR THE HOME
BENEDICTION

This is a Service for married couples who wish to renew their vows. This Ceremony, with slight alterations, may be adapted for use at Wedding Anniversaries.

When the Married Couples are assembled in the Sanctuary at the appointed hour, the Minister shall ascend to the pulpit and begin the service.

OPENING SENTENCES:

Our help is in the name of the Lord, who made heaven and earth. — Psalm 124:8.

Except the Lord build the house, they labour in vain that build it. — Psalm 127:1.

Blessed is every one that feareth the Lord; that walketh in his ways. — Psalm 128:1.

PRAYER:

Almighty God, our heavenly Father, who settest the lonely in families, and causest them to be fruitful and secure: We beseech Thee to have mercy upon us according as we hope in Thee. Grant that Thy presence may be with us on this solemn but joyous occasion as Thou, in Thy Son, wert with those at the marriage in Cana of Galilee, to present to us the best gift, even Thee Thyself; we pray through Jesus Christ our Lord. Amen.

INTRODUCTION TO THE CEREMONY: *(the Minister to the People)*

Dearly beloved, we are assembled here in the presence of God and these friends to witness the renewal of the solemn vows this couple (or N. and N.) made when, as Bride and Groom, they were joined in holy marriage. May they remember with the vividness of this hour the words of the Minister who said that holy matrimony is an honorable estate, instituted of God, blessed by our Lord Jesus Christ, and declared by Paul the Apostle to be honorable among all men.

May we all remember that God has established and sanctified marriage for the welfare and happiness of mankind; that only through holy wedlock are we to people the earth and so establish the family as the foundation of human fellowship. It is for this reason that our Lord and Saviour has declared that a man shall forsake his father and mother and cleave unto his wife. It is for this reason that the Church declares: "Those whom God hath joined together let not man put asunder."

On such a solemn occasion as this — made more so by our marital experiences of weal and woe, of difficulty and conflict, of unexpected changes of circumstances, and of the waxing and waning of the ardor of love and affection — it is fitting that we should seek the divine blessing upon this couple.

PRAYER:

O gracious God, the Father of all mercies and God of grace: We thank Thee for the enrichment and enlargement of life which Thou, in Thy goodness, hast bestowed upon this couple. We pray that Thou wouldst help them now to renew their vows to each other in Thy strength and in Thy fear. Continue them in the faithful discharge of their respective duties as husband and wife, and help them to encourage each other in all godly living and Christian service; through Jesus Christ our Lord. Amen.

RENEWAL OF VOWS:

The Minister (to the Couple)

God has willed that the spiritual bond formed between the two of you in holy marriage be strong — strong and lasting enough to see you through the conflict of ideas, deep disagreements, foolish separations, long or frequent illnesses with their accompanying high cost, the worry of unemployment, underemployment or unemploy-ability itself. It is God's will that this union be strong enough to see you through the worries and responsibilities of parenthood, the burden of debts, deprivations, moral and intellectual failings, the weaknesses and mistakes of each other, retirement, and the inevitable changes in mind and body — all of which may threaten the marriage bond between a husband and wife.

Now, in order to renew your marriage vows, I call upon you in the presence of these witnesses and friends to answer the following questions:

Do you solemnly promise, insofar as you can, to continue to keep the vow and covenant between you made at your wedding?

The Couple:

We do.

The Minister:

Do you promise, insofar as you can, to continue to cultivate love for each other by sympathy, understanding, trustfulness, patience and forbearance, mutual consideration and thoughtfulness?

The Couple:

We do.

The Minister:

Do you promise, insofar as you can, to create a Christian environment in your home, and to encourage each other in godly living and Christian service?

The Couple:

We do.

The Minister:

In token of the pledge you have made to each other and to God in the presence of this company, please join your right hands, and let us pray.

PRAYER FOR THE COUPLE:

Most merciful and gracious God, sanctify and bless these Thy servants, and pour out the riches of Thy grace upon them that, living faithfully together, they may please Thee and live in happy union with each other to their lives' end; through Jesus Christ our Lord. Amen.

PRAYER FOR THE HOME:

We beseech Thee, O Lord God, to bestow Thy blessing upon these Thy servants whom Thou hast appointed to dwell together under the shelter of the same roof, and cause Thy mercies to rest upon their household. Bless their going out and their coming in. Prosper them in all their worthy undertakings; and whether in prosperity or adversity, in health or in sickness, let them know that Thy Fatherly hand is upon them for good. Supply all their needs according to the riches of Thy grace. [Bless the children of their home.] Grant Thy mercy to all those who are dear to them wherever they are, and shelter all Thy children in Thy love; through Jesus Christ our Lord. Amen.

BENEDICTION:

And now may God the Father, the Son, and the Holy Spirit, bless, preserve, and keep you; may the Lord mercifully with His favor look upon you, and fill you with all spiritual benediction and grace; that you may so continue your lives together in this life that in the world to come you may have everlasting life in the presence of God; through our Lord Jesus Christ. Amen.

SERVICE FOR THE DEDICATION OF CHILDREN

OPENING SENTENCES

ADDRESS TO PARENTS

ADDRESS TO PEOPLE

PRAYER OF DEDICATION

DEDICATION OF CHILDREN

PRAYER

BENEDICTION

This Order may be observed at an appropriate time or in connection with a regular service of Morning Worship.

The Parents shall present their Child before the Minister, with the Child's Sponsors (godparents) standing with them.

OPENING SENTENCES:

The mercy of the Lord is from everlasting to everlasting upon them that fear him, and his righteousness unto children's children; to such as keep his covenant, and to those that remember his commandments to do them. — Psalm 103:17-18.

[Thus said the Lord]: Suffer the little children to come unto me, and forbid them not: for of such is the Kingdom of God.... and he took them up in his arms, put his hands upon them, and blessed them. — Mark 10:14, 16.

ADDRESS TO THE PARENTS:

The Minister:

In presenting your Child for dedication to God, do you confess your faith in Jesus Christ as your Lord and Saviour and acknowledge your duty to bring this Child up in the fear and admonition of the Lord, so that *he* may later, of *his* own free choice, confess *his* faith in the Lord Jesus Christ and accept Him as *his* personal Saviour, uniting with the Church through baptism, and dedicating *himself* to the service of God?

The Parents:

We do.

ADDRESS TO THE PEOPLE:

Inasmuch as this responsibility cannot be discharged by the parents alone, and must be shared by all of us since we all, for good or ill, shall exercise influence upon them, God grant that we all shall earnestly assume with these parents the responsibility for the Christian training of *this child* and all children. If you — members of this Church and community — insofar as you can, are willing so to do, then rise and join your hearts with ours in a prayer of dedication of *this child*.

Let us pray:

We offer to Thee *this child,* O gracious, loving Father, as a gift from these parents who, in gratitude having received *him* from Thee, now give *him* back to Thee. So let this be recognized as a symbol of life's demands upon parents concerning their children: As they receive, let them return the gift of their children to life and to Thee. Accept, we pray thee, *this child* whom we now dedicate to Thee. Endow and enrich *him* with Thy heavenly grace. Grant that as *he* grows in stature, *he* may also grow in wisdom and in favor with Thee. Preserve *him* amidst the perils of infancy and childhood; defend *him* amidst the temptations of youth; lead *him* in *his* years of personal accountability to hate the thing which is evil and to choose Thee as *his* portion forever; and bring *him* at last, O God, to Thy heavenly Kingdom; through Jesus Christ our Lord. Amen.

DEDICATION OF THE CHILD:

The Minister: (receives the Child in his arms from the Parent) What is the name of this Child?

The Parent: The Child's name is.........................

The Minister: (laying his hand upon the Child's head)

N., I dedicate thee to God in the Name of the Father, and of the Son, and of the Holy Spirit. Amen. *(The Minister shall then return the Child to the Parent and pray.)*

O merciful and gracious God, our heavenly Father, grant wisdom and patience to these parents that they may wisely and faithfully perform their duty toward *this* child. May they not grow weary or discouraged in a task which may sometimes seem too hard for them. Give them the assurance of Thy constant help and care, we beseech Thee.

Grant Thy counsel and aid to all the parents of this Congregation as they seek to teach and train their children. Help them to lead their households into a more steadfast obedience to Thy will, serving Thee with honor and each other with family devotion; we beseech Thee through Jesus Christ our Lord. Amen.

THE BENEDICTION:

The grace of the Lord Jesus Christ, and the love of God and the communion of the Holy Spirit, be with you all. Amen.

SERVICE FOR THE DEDICATION OF A NEW HOME

OPENING SENTENCES
TALK
PRAYER OF DEDICATION
BENEDICTION

At the time appointed for the Dedication, friends and neighbors having gathered in the new home to celebrate the occasion with the occupants [and their children], the Minister shall observe the following or a similar Order.

OPENING SENTENCES:

Our help is in the name of the Lord, who made heaven and earth. — Psalm 124.8.

Except the Lord build the house, they labour in vain that build it. — Psalm 127:1a.

Let thy mercy, O Lord, be upon us, according as we hope in thee. — Psalm 33:22.

TALK:

My friends, we are met here on this solemn but festive occasion to rejoice with N. and N. *[giving names of the new occupants]* in their commendable accomplishment; to congratulate them; to wish them well; and to unite in prayer for God's blessing on them, [their children] and their new home. It is right that the Christian family should dedicate their home to Almighty God, and implore His protection; for it is in the home that the sanctity of the divine Ordinance of Marriage and the vows that husband and wife have taken are to be religiously guarded. It is in the home that all the children with whom God blesses them are to be nurtured and brought up in the fear and admonition of the Lord. Moreover, the home is to be a place in which Christ may dwell and in which the Christian family may find edification and encouragement in the Christian life. For these and other reasons, let us now join our hearts in prayer for the blessing of Almighty God upon this home and family.

PRAYER OF BENEDICTION:

Most merciful and gracious God, our heavenly Father, we thank Thee for Thy manifold goodness to us Thy children and particularly for the blessing Thou hast bestowed upon this family in granting them possession of this new home. Be pleased to grant them length of days to enjoy this fruit of their labor and sacrifice, and may they, through Thy grace, know the deeper joys of family affection, mutual helpfulness and comfort. May Thy Spirit rest upon this home that it may be protected from dangers without and perils within. When misfortune and adversity, sickness and sorrow, pain and death come, as they inevitably will, be present, O heavenly Father, to heal, to comfort and to bless. Hallow this house for Thy abode, and keep it the place of their earthly rest; through Jesus Christ our Lord, who taught us when we pray to say:

Our Father which are in heaven, Hallowed be thy name. Thy kingdom come. Thy will be done in earth, as it is in heaven. Give us this day our daily bread.

And forgive us our debts, as we forgive our debtors.

And lead us not into temptation, but deliver us from evil: For thine is the kingdom, and the power, and the glory, for ever. Amen.

BENEDICTION:

The peace of God, which passeth all understanding, keep your hearts and minds in the knowledge and love of God and of his son Jesus Christ our Lord: and the blessing of God Almighty, the Father, the Son, and the Holy Spirit, rest upon you and abide with you for ever. Amen.

SECTION FOUR

The Burial of the Dead

GUIDING PRINCIPLES AND PRACTICAL SUGGESTIONS

Whether in public or in private the burial of the dead should be attended with the greatest solemnity and dignity and with respectable brevity. This is no occasion for a "program," for eloquence or display, but a time to eulogize the dead, comfort the mourners, exhort the living, and to bow in humble submission to the inevitable facts of life.

The burial of the Christian dead should be a Christian rite. No heathenish practices, however innocently suggested, should be permitted.

Since the Minister and Officiant at the funeral rite has a responsibility to the living as well as the dead, his text, scriptures and hymns should be selected with the uttermost appropriateness. Especially should this be the case at the funeral service which makes more than ordinary demands upon the Minister or presents special problems.

The Minister should discourage the excessive use and display of flowers at the funeral service but should encourage friends of the deceased to invest in a living memorial to the dead. Such memorials could be gifts to the deceased's favorite charity or organization, a financial contribution or some other valuable aid to a cause in which he was deeply interested, his Church or some other institution with which he sustained a relationship. Contributions to the welfare of his family, if this be a need, would not be out of order if proffered prudently.

The Minister's ministry to the bereaved should extend beyond a visit to the home upon the decease of a member of the family, the conduct of the funeral service, and the trip to the cemetery. His greatest, and, perhaps, most needed ministry may be performed by a visit to the home of the bereaved when the service is over and

all the friends are gone. If he cannot make the visit, a telephone
call, expressing concern and giving reassurance of God's presence
to comfort, will not be without real benefit to them.

SERVICE FOR THE BURIAL OF AN ADULT

Procession
Prayer
Music
Scripture Reading
Music
[Condolences, Resolutions, Obituary]*
Eulogy and Prayer
Recession
Grave-Side Service
   Sentences
   The Committal and Prayer
   Benediction

Procession: (*The following Scripture is recited by the Minister
as he leads the Procession into the Sanctuary.*)

I am the resurrection, and the life [saith the Lord]: he that
believeth in me, though he were dead, yet shall he live: And
whosoever liveth and believeth in me shall never die. — John
11:25-26.

The eternal God is thy refuge, and underneath are the everlasting arms. — Deuteronomy 33:27.

Blessed be God, even the Father of our Lord Jesus Christ, the
Father of mercies, and the God of all comfort. — II Corinthians
1:3.

Prayer:

Almighty God, source of all comfort and our peace in dying:
We thank Thee for Thy Son Jesus Christ who through Thy

*Items in brackets are optional.

grace and power hath brought life and immortality to light, so that in our frailty we may seek Thy strength and, in our sorrow, Thy comfort. Help us now to put our trust in Thee that we may obtain the blessing of Thy grace, the comfort of Thy peace and the patience of eternal hope; through Jesus Christ our Lord. Amen.

MUSIC: *(a Hymn, Solo or an Anthem)*

SCRIPTURE READING

From the Psalter

The Lord is my shepherd; I shall not want.

He maketh me to lie down in green pastures: he leadeth me beside the still waters.

He restoreth my soul: he leadeth me in the paths of righteousness for his name's sake.

Yea, though I walk through the valley of the shadow of death, I will fear no evil: for thou art with me; thy rod and thy staff they comfort me.

Thou preparest a table before me in the presence of mine enemies: thou anointest my head with oil; my cup runneth over.

Surely goodness and mercy shall follow me all the days of my life: and I will dwell in the house of the Lord for ever. — Psalm 23.

— or —

Come, ye children, hearken unto me: I will teach you the fear of the Lord.

What man is he that desireth life, and loveth many days, that he may see good?

Keep thy tongue from evil, and thy lips from speaking guile.

Depart from evil, and do good; seek peace, and pursue it.

The eyes of the Lord are upon the righteous, and his ears are open unto their cry.

The face of the Lord is against them that do evil, to cut off the remembrance of them from the earth.

The Lord is nigh unto them that are of a broken heart; and saveth such as be of a contrite spirit.

Many are the afflictions of the righteous: but the Lord delivereth him out of them all.

He keepeth all his bones: not one of them is broken.

The Lord redeemeth the soul of his servants: and none of them that trust in him shall be desolate. — Psalm 34:11-16, 18-20, 22.

From the New Testament

Let not your heart be troubled: ye believe in God, believe also in me.

In my Father's house are many mansions: if it were not so, I would have told you. I go to prepare a place for you.

And if I go and prepare a place for you, I will come again, and receive you unto myself; that where I am, there ye may be also.

I will not leave you comfortless: I will come to you.

Yet a little while, and the world seeth me no more; but ye see me: because I live, ye shall live also.

Peace I leave with you, my peace I give unto you: not as the world giveth, give I unto you. Let not your heart be troubled, neither let it be afraid. — John 14:1-3, 18-19, 27.

— *or* —

If in this life only we have hope in Christ, we are of all men most miserable.

But now is Christ risen from the dead, and become the first fruits of them that slept.

For since by man came death, by man came also the resurrection of the dead.

For as in Adam all die, even so in Christ shall all be made alive.

But every man in his own order: Christ the firstfruits; afterward they that are Christ's at his coming.

Then cometh the end, when he shall have delivered up the kingdom to God, even the Father; when he shall have put down all rule and all authority and power.

For he must reign, till he hath put all enemies under his feet.

The last enemy that shall be destroyed is death. — I Corinthians 15:19-26.

— or —

Who shall separate us from the love of Christ? shall tribulation, or distress, or persecution, or famine, or nakedness, or peril, or sword?

As it is written, For thy sake we are killed all the day long; we are accounted as sheep for the slaughter.

Nay, in all these things we are more than conquerors through him that loved us.

For I am persuaded, that neither death, nor life, nor angels, nor principalities, nor powers, nor things present, nor things to come,

Nor height, nor death, nor any other creature, shall be able to separate us from the love of God, which is in Christ Jesus our Lord. — Romans 8:35-39.

— or —

And I saw a new heaven and a new earth: for the first heaven and the first earth were passed away; and there was no more sea.

And I John saw the holy city, new Jerusalem, coming down from God out of heaven, prepared as a bride adorned for her husband.

And I heard a great voice out of heaven saying, Behold, the tabernacle of God is with men, and he will dwell with them, and they shall be his people, and God himself shall be with them, and be their God.

And God shall wipe away all tears from their eyes; and there shall be no more death, neither sorrow, nor crying, neither shall there be any more pain: for the former things are passed away.

And he that sat upon the throne said, Behold, I make all things new.

He that overcometh shall inherit all things; and I will be his God, and he shall be my son. — Revelation 21:1-5a, 7.

MUSIC:

Here may be sung a Hymn, Solo or an Anthem, followed by the ACKNOWLEDGEMENT OF CONDOLENCES *on behalf of the be-*

reaved family, the reading of SPECIAL RESOLUTIONS *and the* OBITUARY. *The latter acts may be omitted if desired. In that event, the* EULOGY *would be given immediately after the afore-mentioned music instead of following the* OBITUARY. *The* EULOGY *shall be concluded with a Prayer in the following or similar words.*

PRAYER:

Our gracious heavenly Father: We beseech Thee to grant unto all who are bereaved the faith and strength hopefully to endure the departure of their loved one from this earthly life. May they serenely face the days to come with deepened trust in Thee. Give to them the power to live in greater faithfulness to the life of that unseen world where the souls of the righteous are in peace and the eternal ties of those we have lost awhile bind us in sacred remembrance and love to them. Keep us, O heavenly Father, in fellowship with all who wait for Thee in joyful expectation of an endless life; through Jesus Christ our Lord. Amen.

— *or* —

O Thou who art the God of all comfort: Look with compassion upon these who are at this time bereaved, and whose hearts are heavy with grief. May the tie that has been broken on earth bind them closer to Thee and to each other. Grant that they may be brought, through this experience, to offer themselves in dedication to Thy service, submitting themselves in patience and trust to Thy holy will; through Jesus Christ our Lord. Amen.

RECESSION: (*The Minister shall now lead the Recession out of the Sanctuary, saying one or more verses from Holy Scripture. The Service is continued at the Cemetery.*)

GRAVE-SIDE SERVICE:

At the Cemetery, the Minister shall lead the way to the Grave and take his position at its head. When the family and friends are assembled, the Minister shall say one or more Sentences from the Holy Scriptures.

Sentences:

I am he that liveth, and was dead [saith the Lord]; and, behold, I am alive for evermore, Amen. — Revelation 1:18.

There remaineth therefore a rest to the people of God. — Hebrews 4:9.

And this is the promise that he hath promised us, even eternal life. — I John 2:25.

(Then shall the Minister commit the body.)

The Committal:

And now unto the mercy of Almighty God, we commend the spirit of our departed *brother* and commit *his* body to the ground:* earth to earth, ashes to ashes, dust to dust; looking for the general resurrection at the last day when those who die in the Lord shall be raised to eternal glory and an endless life of joy and peace with God; through our Lord Jesus Christ. Amen.

Blessed are the dead which die in the Lord from henceforth: Yea, saith the Spirit, that they may rest from their labours; and their works do follow them. — Revelation 14:13.

(The following Committal may be used for those who have died outside of the fellowship of the Church):

Forasmuch as the spirit of the departed has entered into the life immortal, we therefore commit *his* body to the ground:* earth to earth, ashes to ashes, dust to dust; but his spirit we commend unto the mercy of Almighty God, who doth not deal with us after our sins nor reward us according to our iniquities. Amen.

Prayer:

O Lord God, our compassionate Father, who alone canst heal the broken in heart and bind up their wounds: Grant unto Thy sorrowing children the peace and comfort of Thy loving care, we beseech Thee, so that, with patience and trust in Thee, they may learn to abide the changes and the losses of this mortal life and the afflictions with which we are afflicted in this world. Give to them Thy sustaining grace that they

His body to the deep (in case of a burial at sea), or *his* ashes to their final resting place (in case of cremation).

may live in hope of the life everlasting and be granted to consummate their lives in peace with Thee; through Jesus Christ our Lord. Amen.

— or —

Eternal God, Thou who art from everlasting to everlasting: Cause everyone of us to consider the uncertainty of life that we may live in readiness for Thy call to us. May the day of Thy return be a day of welcome and gladness. Enable us, by the gracious indwelling of the Holy Spirit, to continue in faith and in Thy service to the end of our earthly days that we may reign with Thee throughout eternity; through Jesus Christ our Lord. Amen.

Benediction:

Now unto him that is able to keep you from falling, and to present you faultless before the presence of his glory with exceeding joy, To the only wise God our Saviour, be glory and majesty, dominion and power, both now and ever. Amen. — Jude 24-25.

SERVICE FOR THE BURIAL OF A YOUNG PERSON

PROCESSION
MUSIC
SCRIPTURE READING
[MUSIC]*
[BRIEF MESSAGE]
PRAYER
RECESSION
GRAVE-SIDE SERVICE
    SENTENCES
    COMMITTAL AND PRAYER
    BENEDICTION

*Items in brackets are optional.

When this Service is conducted at the Church, there shall be a Procession with the Minister saying one or more Sentences from Holy Scripture as he leads the way. Otherwise the Sentences may be said from a speaker's stand.

SENTENCES:

So teach us to number our days, that we may apply our hearts unto wisdom. — Psalm 90:12.

He shall feed his flock like a shepherd: he shall gather the lambs with his arm, and carry them in his bosom, and shall gently lead those that are with young. — Isaiah 40:11.

PRAYER:

Almighty God, our loving heavenly Father, who makest no life in vain but lovest all whom Thou hast created: Solace us Thy children in our sorrow and banish the darkness which afflicts us in our loss of a loved one so young. Help us amidst the trials and the temptation of the moment to preserve within us that childlike faith and trust which entertains no doubt of Thy love or Thy care. So comfort and strengthen us now that neither sorrow nor the shock of a seemingly untimely death shall have dominion over us; we pray through Jesus Christ our Lord, even Thine only begotten Son. Amen.

MUSIC: *(a Hymn or Solo)*

SCRIPTURE READING:

From the Old Testament

Lord, make me to know mine end, and the measure of my days, what it is; that I may know how frail I am.

Behold, thou hast made my days as an handbreadth; and mine age is as nothing before thee: verily every man at his best state is altogether vanity. — Psalm 39:4-5.

— *or* —

It is of the Lord's mercies that we are not consumed, because his compassions fail not.

They are new every morning: great is thy faithfulness.

The Lord is good unto them that wait for him, to the soul that seeketh him. — Lamentations 3:22-23, 25.

But though he cause grief, yet will he have compassion according to the multitude of his mercies.

For he doth not afflict willingly nor grieve the children of men. — Lamentations 3:32-33.

— *or* —

I will lift up mine eyes unto the hills, from whence cometh my help.

My help cometh from the Lord, which made heaven and earth.

He will not suffer thy foot to be moved: he that keepeth thee will not slumber.

Behold, he that keepeth Israel shall neither slumber nor sleep.

The Lord is thy keeper: the Lord is thy shade upon thy right hand.

The sun shall not smite thee by day, nor the moon by night.

The Lord shall preserve thee from all evil: he shall preserve thy soul.

The Lord shall preserve thy going out and thy coming in from this time forth, and even for evermore. — Psalm 121.

From the New Testament

At the same time came the disciples unto Jesus, saying, Who is the greatest in the kingdom of heaven?

And Jesus called a little child unto him, and set him in the midst of them,

And said, Verily I say unto you, Except ye be converted, and become as little children, ye shall not enter into the kingdom of heaven.

Whosoever therefore shall humble himself as this little child, the same is greatest in the kingdom of heaven.

And whoso shall receive one such little child in my name receiveth me.

Take heed that ye despise not one of these little ones; for I say unto you, That in heaven their angels do always behold the face of my Father which is in heaven.

Even so it is not the will of your Father, which is in heaven, that one of these little ones should perish. — Matthew 18:1-5, 10, 14.

— or —

But when Jesus saw it, he was much displeased, and said unto them, Suffer the little children to come unto me, and forbid them not: for of such is the kingdom of God.

Verily I say unto you, Whosoever shall not receive the kingdom of God as a little child, he shall not enter therein.

And he took them up in his arms, put his hands upon them, and blessed them. — Mark 10:14-16.

— or —

For whether we live, we live unto the Lord; and whether we die, we die unto the Lord: whether we live therefore, or die, we are the Lord's. — Romans 14:8.

For here have we no continuing city, but we seek one to come. — Hebrews 13:14.

[MUSIC]: *(a Hymn or Solo)*

[BRIEF MESSAGE]:

PRAYER:

O Thou who art the God of all comfort: Look with compassion upon these who are at this time bereaved, and whose hearts are heavy with grief. May the tie that has been broken on earth bind them closer to Thee, to their loved one in heaven, and to each other. Grant that they may offer themselves in dedication to Thy service, submitting themselves in patience and trust to Thy Holy will.

Cause everyone of us, O God, to consider the uncertainty of life that we may live in readiness for Thy call to us. May the day of Thy return be a day of welcome and gladness. Enable us, by the gracious indwelling of the Holy Spirit, to continue in faith and in Thy service to the end of our earthly days that we may reign with Thee throughout eternity; through Jesus Christ our Lord. Amen.

RECESSION: *(The Minister shall now lead the Recession out of the Sanctuary, saying one or more verses from Holy Scripture. The Service is continued at the Cemetery.)*

At the Cemetery, the Minister shall lead the way to the Grave and take his position at its head. When the family and friends are assembled, the Minister shall say one or more Sentences from Holy Scripture.

Sentences:

Our help is in the name of the Lord, who made heaven and earth. — Psalm 124:8.

Blessed are the pure in heart: for they shall see God. — Matthew 5:8.

But the mercy of the Lord is from everlasting to everlasting upon them that fear him, and his righteousness unto children's children. — Psalm 103:17.

(Then shall the Minister commit the Body.)

The Committal:

And now unto the mercy of Almighty God, we commend the spirit of this departed child and commit *his* body to the ground: earth to earth, ashes to ashes, dust to dust; looking for the general resurrection at the last day when those who die in the Lord shall be raised to eternal glory and an endless life of joy and peace with God; through our Lord Jesus Christ. Amen.

Blessed are the dead who die in the Lord from henceforth: yea, saith the Spirit, that they may rest from their labours; and their works, do follow them. — Revelation 14:13.

Prayer:

O merciful and everloving God, our heavenly Father: We commend to Thee all of these Thy children for Thy holy keeping. Lead them to walk in righteousness and be with them in their temptations. Confirm, comfort and sustain them, and bring them at last to Thy heavenly rest; through Jesus Christ our Lord. Amen.

Benediction:

The grace of the Lord Jesus Christ, and the love of God, and the communion of the Holy Spirit, be with you all. Amen.

SERVICE FOR A PERSON WHO HAS COMMITTED SUICIDE

OPENING SENTENCES

INVOCATION

MUSIC

PRAYER

MUSIC

[EULOGY]*

PRAYER

RECESSION

AT GRAVE

   SENTENCES

   THE COMMITTAL

   PRAYER

   BENEDICTION

The bereaved family should make the decision whether the Service for a loved one who has committed suicide is to be private or public. The Minister might inadvertently increase rather than relieve the mourners' burden by advising a private service. The private service may or may not be in the best interest of the bereaved family. Sometimes the private service held upon the advice of Minister or friends has an adverse rather than a beneficial effect upon the bereaved family. The very privacy of the service may suggest a disgrace imposed upon the family by a member's self-destruction. A transfer of guilt upon the bereaved family and a feeling of rejection by friends, the community, and the Church may result from an ill-advised private service and make the mourners' grief far more intense than it otherwise would be.

Suicide, it should be understood, is regarded by the general public as the extreme in tragedy, even though the rate of its frequency has increased markedly in modern times. Moreover, the fact that persons of well-known integrity and altruistic purposes, with

*Items in brackets are optional.

whose lives no opprobrium is connected, are occasional victims of
self-destruction, complicates our understanding and handling of a
very complex problem and greatly increases the demands of grief-
work for the families thus involved. The Minister should seek to
provide a supportive force through his several ministries for families
so bereaved as his best contribution to their inner strength and
comfort and his wisest and most effective action upon a difficult
problem.

The public service has a supportive value to the bereaved which
the private service does not have. It is the family and not the deceased who need the public support and sympathetic understanding of friends and the fellowship of love in such an hour. It should
also be recognized that often some members of the bereaved family
are faithful members of the Church, even if the deceased is not,
and they should have the full support of their Church. They
should not be abandoned in such an hour or sympathized with
only privately, if what they need is public support in their sorrow.

*The Minister shall say one or more of the following Sentences
from Holy Scripture during the Procession, if the Service is public,
or as the Opening Sentences, if the Service is private.*

OPENING SENTENCES:

I am the resurrection, and the life [saith the Lord]: he that
believeth in me, though he were dead, yet shall he live: And
whosoever liveth and believeth in me shall never die. — John
11:25-26.

The Lord is merciful and gracious, slow to anger, and plenteous in mercy. — Psalm 103:8.

It is of the Lord's mercies that we are not consumed, because
his compassions fail not. — Lamentations 3:22.

INVOCATION:

O holy and benign God our Father, who art full of compassion
and plenteous in mercy: Grant to us Thy children the strength
and the comfort of the Holy Spirit in our hour of loss and grief,
so that no distress of mind may enthrall our spirits and no sorrow turn us from continually seeking after Thee. Direct and
support us in our grief and fill our hearts with Thy peace;
through Jesus Christ our Lord. Amen.

MUSIC: *(a Hymn such as one of the following)*
　　"I Know Not What the Future Hath"
　　"O Lord of Life Where'er They Be"
　　"God of Our Life, Through All the Circling Years"
　　"O God, Our Help in Ages Past"

SCRIPTURE READING:

From the Old Testament

Man that is born of a woman is of few days, and full of trouble.

He cometh forth like a flower, and is cut down: he fleeth also as a shadow, and continueth not.

And dost thou open thine eyes upon such an one, and bringest me into judgment with thee?

As the waters fail from the sea, and the flood decayeth and drieth up:

So man lieth down, and riseth not: till the heavens be no more, they shall not awake, nor be raised out of their sleep.

O that thou wouldest hide me in the grave, that thou wouldest keep me secret, until thy wrath be past, that thou wouldest appoint me a set time, and remember me!

If a man die, shall he live again? all the days of my appointed time will I wait, till my change come. — Job 14: 1-3, 11-14.

— *or* —

O Lord, thou hast searched me, and known me.

Thou knowest my downsitting and mine uprising, thou understandest my thought afar off.

Thou compassest my path and my lying down, and art acquainted with all my ways.

For there is not a word in my tongue, but, lo, O Lord, thou knowest it altogether.

Thou hast beset me behind and before, and laid thine hand up me.

Such knowledge is too wonderful for me; it is high, I cannot attain unto it.

Whither shall I go from thy spirit? or whither shall I flee from thy presence?

If I ascend up into heaven, thou art there: if I make my bed in hell, behold, thou art there.

If I take the wings of the morning, and dwell in the uttermost parts of the sea;

Even there shall thy hand lead me, and thy right hand shall hold me.

If I say, Surely the darkness shall cover me; even the night shall be light about me.

Yea, the darkness hideth not from thee; but the night shineth as the day: the darkness and the light are both alike to thee.

For thou hast possessed my reins: thou hast covered me in my mother's womb.

I will praise thee; for I am fearfully and wonderfully made: marvellous are thy works; and that my soul knoweth right well.

My substance was not hid from thee, when I was made in secret, and curiously wrought in the lowest parts of the earth.

Thine eyes did see my substance, yet being unperfect; and in thy book all my members were written, which in continuance were fashioned, when as yet there was none of them.

How precious also are thy thoughts unto me, O God! how great is the sum of them!

Search me, O God, and know my heart: try me, and know my thoughts:

And see if there be any wicked way in me, and lead me in the way everlasting. — Psalm 139:1-17, 23-24.

From the New Testament

Let not your heart be troubled [saith the Lord]: ye believe in God, believe also in me. — John 14:1.

But the Comforter, which is the Holy Ghost, whom the Father will send in my name, he shall teach you all things, and bring all things to your remembrance, whatsoever I have said to you.

Peace I leave with you, my peace I give unto you: not as the world giveth, give I unto you. Let not your heart be troubled, neither let it be afraid. — John 14:26-27.

Be of good cheer; I have overcome the world. — John 16:33.

— or —

If in this life only we have hope in Christ, we are of all men most miserable.

But now is Christ risen from the dead, and become the first-fruits of them that slept.

For since by man came death, by man came also the resurrection of the dead.

For as in Adam all die, even so in Christ shall all be made alive. — I Corinthians 15:19-22.

For God hath not appointed us to wrath, but to obtain salvation by our Lord Jesus Christ,

Who died for us, that, whether we wake or sleep, we should live together with him. — I Thessalonians 5:9-10.

Seeing then that we have a great high priest, that is passed into the heavens, Jesus the Son of God, let us hold fast our profession.

For we have not an high priest which cannot be touched with the feeling of our infirmities; but was in all points tempted like as we are, yet without sin.

Let us therefore come boldly unto the throne of grace, that we may obtain mercy, and find grace to help in time of need. — Hebrews 4:14-16.

— or —

And I saw a new heaven and a new earth: for the first heaven and the first earth were passed away; and there was no more sea.

And I John saw the holy city, new Jerusalem, coming down from God out of heaven, prepared as a bride adorned for her husband.

And I heard a great voice out of heaven saying, Behold, the tabernacle of God is with men, and he will dwell with them, and they shall be his people, and God himself shall be with them and be their God.

And God shall wipe away all tears from their eyes; and there shall be no more death, neither sorrow, nor crying, neither shall there be any more pain: for the former things are passed away.

And he that sat upon the throne said, Behold, I make all things new. And he said unto me, Write: for these words are true and faithful. — Revelation 21:1-5.

MUSIC: *(a Solo, an Anthem, or a Hymn such as one of the following)*

"Come, Ye Disconsolate, Where'er Ye Languish"
"From Every Stormy Wind That Blows"
"My Times Are in Thy Hands"
"Guide Me, O Thou Great Jehovah"

PRAYER: *(beginning with the frailty of man and the sorrow we experience in the loss of a loved one, but emphasizing the compassion and mercy, and the grace and power of God in Christ, in these or similar words)*

Almighty and everlasting God, our heavenly Father, who surroundest our brief moments upon this earth with the eternity of Thy love and care and makest man's frailty the object of Thy compassion and mercy: Make us to know our end, and the measure of our days, what it is; that we may kow how frail we are. Regard with pity our weak, disquieted spirits in this time of sorrow, for we cannot sustain our loss or conquer our grief without the aid of Thy Holy Spirit.

O God who didst make us and who alone knowest our frame: Thou knowest what is in us better than we ourselves can know. Thou seest and understandest the inward devices we unconsciously create to face or to reject the demands of our daily lives. We are often unaware of the deaths we die or the lives we live many times before our earthly existence ends. We often do not realize how deep and hidden are many forces that lie within us, waiting to overpower us when the right circumstances or conditions prevail. We often do not know how great and potentially dangerous are the inadequacies and the deficiencies with which we were born and how great or small our helplessness really is. But Thou, O God, art the strength of our lives and the preserver of our souls.

Our merciful Saviour and compassionate God, with whom alone the souls of men may truly be entrusted: Reveal to us anew the mighty working of Thy grace and power in Thy Son Jesus Christ, who descended into hell and on the third day rose again from the dead and ascended into heaven where He now sitteth on the right hand of God the Father from whence He shall come to judge the quick and the dead. Assure us that the souls of those who depart from this life are committed unto Thy everlasting mercy.

O great and eternal God, our thoughts are not Thy thoughts and how unsearchable is Thy understanding. Judge us Thyself and plead our cause. Consider the helpless estate of Thy children. Preserve us and uphold all those who hope in Thee; through Jesus Christ our Lord. Amen.

MUSIC: *(a Hymn such as one of the following)*
   "There's a Wideness in God's Mercy"
   "God Is Love; His Mercy Brightens"
   "O God, in Whom We Live and Move"
   "O Son of God Incarnate"

[EULOGY]:

PRAYER:

Our gracious heavenly Father, we beseech Thee to grant to all who are bereaved the faith and strength hopefully to endure the departure of their loved one from this earthly life. May they serenely face the days to come with deepened trust in Thee and an assurance of the supportive power of friends, the Church and the Holy Spirit; through Jesus Christ our Lord. Amen.

RECESSION: *(The Minister shall now lead the Recession out of the Sanctuary or Chapel, saying one or more Sentences from Holy Scripture. The Service is continued at the Cemetery.)*

GRAVE-SIDE SERVICE:

At the Cemetery, the Minister shall lead the way to the Grave and take his position at its head. When the family and friends are assembled, the Minister shall say one or more Sentences from Holy Scripture.

Sentences:

I am he that liveth, and was dead [saith the Lord]; and, behold, I am alive for evermore, Amen; and have the keys of hell and of death. — Revelation 1:18.

Blessed be God, even the Father of our Lord Jesus Christ, the Father of mercies, and the God of all comfort. — II Corinthians 1:3.

(Then shall the Minister commit the body.)

The Committal:

Forasmuch as the spirit of the departed has entered into the life immortal, we therefore commit *his* body to the ground:* earth to earth, ashes to ashes, dust to dust; but his spirit we commend unto the mercy of Almighty God.

Prayer:

O Lord God, our compassionate heavenly Father, we commend to Thy keeping the souls of all these Thy children that make up this company that they may have the assurance of Thy presence to inspire, Thy power to preserve and Thy support in holy, confident living. Forsake not the lonely and leave not the sorrowful in grief. Give to those who feel desolate useful, meaningful things to do and return the bereaved in hope and faith to the new opportunities and their continuing tasks at home; through Jesus Christ our Lord. Amen.

Benediction:

And the very God of peace sanctify you wholly; and I pray God your whole spirit and soul and body be preserved blameless unto the coming of our Lord Jesus Christ. Faithful is he that calleth you; who also will do it. The grace of our Lord Jesus Christ be with you. Amen. — I Thessalonians 5:23-24, 28.

---

*His body to the deep (in case of a burial at sea), or *his* ashes to their final resting place (in case of cremation).

SCRIPTURAL TEXTS

FOR GENERAL USE

God took him. — Genesis 5:24.

If a man die, shall he live again? — Job 14:14.

Lord, make me to know mine end, and the measure of my days, what it is; that I may know how frail I am. — Psalm 39:4.

So teach us to number our days, that we may apply our hearts unto wisdom. — Psalm 90:12.

As for man, his days are as grass; as a flower of the field, so he flourisheth. — Psalm 103:15.

He giveth his beloved sleep. — Psalm 127:2.

Well done, thou good and faithful servant. — Matthew 25:21.

The night cometh. — John 9:4.

Jesus said unto her, I am the resurrection, and the life. — John 11:25.

To them who by patient continuance in well doing seek for glory and honour and immortality, eternal life. — Romans 2:7.

If in this life only we have hope in Christ, we are of all men most miserable. — I Corinthians 15:19.

Death is swallowed up in victory. — I Corinthians 15:54.

He looked for a city which hath foundations, whose builder and maker is God. — Hebrews 11:10.

Blessed are the dead which die in the Lord. — Revelation 14:13.

Blessed are they that do his commandments, that they may have right to the tree of life. — Revelation 22:14.

FOR A CHILD

Is it well with the child? And she answered, It is well. — II Kings 4:26.

He shall gather the lambs with his arm, and carry them in his bosom. — Isaiah 40:11.

And the streets of the city shall be full of boys and girls playing in the streets thereof. — Zechariah 8:5.

Suffer little children . . . to come unto me. — Matthew 19:14.

Of such is the kingdom of heaven. — Matthew 19:14.

For a Youth

And Pharaoh said unto Jacob, How old art thou? — Genesis 47:8.

He did that which was right in the sight of the Lord, and walked in the ways of David his father, and declined neither to the right hand, nor to the left. — II Chronicles 34:2.

Rejoice, O young man, in thy youth; and let thy heart cheer thee in the days of thy youth, and walk in the ways of thine heart, and in the sight of thine eyes: but know thou, that for all these things God will bring thee into judgment. — Ecclesiastes 11:9.

Even the youths shall faint and be weary, and the young men shall utterly fall. — Isaiah 40:30.

It is good for a man that he bear the yoke in his youth. — Lamentations 3:27.

He that overcometh shall inherit all things; and I will be his God and he shall be my son. — Revelation 21:7.

For an Aged Person

And died in a good old age, an old man, and full of years; and was gathered to his people. — Genesis 25:8.

Thou shalt come to thy grave in a full age, like as a shock of corn cometh in his season. — Job 5:26.

And even to your old age I am he; and even to hoar hairs will I carry you: I have made, and I will bear; even I will carry, and will deliver you. — Isaiah 46:4.

As the days of a tree are the days of my people, and mine elect shall long enjoy the work of their hands. — Isaiah 65:22.

Having a desire to depart, and to be with Christ; which is far better. — Philippians 1:23.

For a Victim of Tragic or Sudden Death

The secret things belong unto the Lord our God. — Deuteronomy 29:29.

When I thought to know this, it was too painful for me. — Psalm 73:16.

Boast not thyself of tomorrow; for thou knowest not what a day may bring forth. — Proverbs 27:1.

Be ye also ready. — Matthew 24:44.

Watch therefore, for ye know neither the day nor the hour wherein the Son of man cometh. — Matthew 25:13.

Think ye that they were sinners above all men that dwelt in Jerusalem? I tell you, Nay. — Luke 13:4-5.

I reckon that the sufferings of this present time are not worthy to be compared with the glory which shall be revealed in us. — Romans 8:18.

FOR A PERSON OUTSIDE THE FELLOWSHIP OF THE CHURCH

For the Lord is good; his mercy is everlasting; and his truth endureth to all generations. — Psalm 100:5.

He will regard the prayer of the destitute, and not despise their prayer. — Psalm 102:17.

The Lord is merciful and gracious, slow to anger, and plenteous in mercy. — Psalm 103:8.

He hath not dealt with us after our sins; nor rewarded us according to our iniquities. — Psalm 103:10.

Nevertheless he regarded their affliction, when he heard their cry. — Psalm 106:44.

Not everyone that saith unto me, Lord, Lord, shall enter into the kingdom of heaven; but he that doeth the will of my Father which is in heaven. — Matthew 7:21.

The tree is known by his fruit. — Matthew 12:33.

Other sheep I have, which are not of this fold: them also I must bring, and they shall hear my voice. — John 10:16.

SECTION FIVE

Special Occasions

GUIDING PRINCIPLES AND PRACTICAL SUGGESTIONS

The Minister, in his office as pastor of a local church, must perform many functions and be knowledgeable about many things with respect to the perpetuation, the continuing vitality, the spiritual growth, and the doctrinal purity of the Church as an institution. Under his leadership, lay persons must be constantly discovered, recruited, trained and dedicated for service in significant and essential ministries of the Church; men must be inspired to hear the call of God in Christ to the Gospel Ministry and to accept responsibility for their intellectual and spiritual preparation with a view to being ordained either for charges of their own or for some other responsible position in the Church; and new churches may be organized and dedicated.

These responsibilities should be regarded as a holy charge by our Lord and Christ — a charge not to be taken lightly or performed carelessly. While the minister is not God and cannot judge the hearts and minds of men, yet he must insist upon a faithful compliance by all members with what he knows through the body of truth, established practices, and Faith and Order of his Church, to be divinely inspired and approved rules, standards and procedures for perpetuating, strengthening and preserving the Church not only as an assembly of the people of God but as the Body of Christ.

The Minister must also feel a deep responsibility for establishing and maintaining comity and a cooperative unity among the ministers and churches of the various faiths to the end that God may be glorified and the work of the Lord advanced and blessed.

SERVICE FOR RECEPTION OF NEW CONVERTS INTO FULL MEMBERSHIP

OPENING SENTENCES AND INVOCATION

HYMN

TEN COMMANDMENTS AND SUMMARY

HYMN

BEATITUDES

PRAYER

HYMN

BRIEF SERMON AND REAFFIRMATION OF VOWS

   ADDRESS TO CONGREGATION AND CONVERTS

   RIGHT HAND OF FELLOWSHIP AND HYMN

THE LORD'S SUPPER

   INTRODUCTORY WORDS

   PRAYER

   DISTRIBUTION OF BREAD AND WINE

HYMN

BENEDICTION

The evangelical church should always emphasize the importance of decision and commitment and church membership to converts. This should be done through special classes organized for this purpose, culminating in a public rite when Converts are received into full church membership. This Order should be a separate Service in which the whole congregation participates.

At the hour appointed for the Service, the Minister shall enter the Sanctuary, finding the Converts seated before him, and say one or more Sentences from Holy Scripture. The Congregation shall stand through the singing of the first Hymn.

OPENING SENTENCES:

O taste and see that the Lord is good: blessed is the man that trusteth in him. — Psalm 34:8.

Him that cometh to me I will in no wise cast out. — John 6:37.

He that cometh to God must believe that he is, and that he is a rewarder of them that diligently seek him. — Hebrews 11:6.

INVOCATION:

Our heavenly Father, prepare our hearts for worshiping Thee and for calling upon Thy name aright. Meet us here, O God, and make Thyself known to us in song and prayer and in Thy Word. Let us all rejoice and be glad in Thy house; through our Lord and Saviour Jesus Christ. Amen.

HYMN: (a Hymn of praise, such as one of the following)

"Fairest Lord Jesus"
"Shepherd of Eager Youth"
"How Sweet the Name of Jesus Sounds"
"Praise the Lord, His Glories Show"
"Holy, Holy, Holy, Lord God Almighty"

TEN COMMANDMENTS AND SUMMARY:

(See page 33 of this book.)

HYMN: (a Hymn of the Gospel, such as one of the following)

"Tell Me the Old, Old Story"
"Break Thou the Bread of Life"
"Sing Them Over Again to Me"
"Tell Me the Story of Jesus"
"I Think when I Read That Sweet Story of Old"

THE BEATITUDES:

(See page 35 of this book.)

PRAYER: (a petition for light and understanding and full devotion to God through His Holy Spirit, followed by the Lord's Prayer in concert)

Our gracious heavenly Father, the Father of our Lord and Saviour Jesus Christ, in whose wisdom Thy children become wise and by whose strength we become strong: Open our minds to understand Thy Word and open our hearts to receive it. May we in deep sincerity and full devotion offer our lives a living sacrifice, holy and acceptable unto Thee. May we honor Thee, love our Christ, respect and be loyal to our Church;

through Jesus Christ our Lord, who taught us when we pray to say:

Our Father which art in heaven, Hallowed by Thy name. Thy kingdom come. Thy will be done in earth, as it is in heaven. Give us this day our daily bread. And forgive us our debts, as we forgive our debtors. And lead us not into temptation, but deliver us from evil: For Thine is the kingdom, and the power, and the glory, for ever. Amen.

HYMN: (*a Hymn of consecration or aspiration, such as one of the following, the congregation standing*)

"Dear Master, in Whose Life I See"
"O Master, Let Me Walk with Thee"
"O Jesus, I Have Promised"
"Living for Jesus a Life That Is True"
"Just As I Am, Thine Own to Be"
"Take My Life, and Let It Be"

BRIEF SERMON:

A Brief Address shall now be given, after which the Church Clerk shall read the names of all Converts to be received into full membership of the Church. They shall stand as their name is called. Then shall the Minister address the Congregation and Converts in turn.

REAFFIRMATION OF VOWS:

Address to Congregation and Converts:

The Minister: (to the Congregation)

These persons, by the act of baptism, have been received into the Church. The proper subjects of baptism are believers, and entrance into the visible Church on the part of new believers is baptism. We are assembled here publicly to welcome them to the full rights, privileges and responsibilities of Church membership by extending to them the Right Hand of Fellowship.

The Minister: (to the Converts)

By baptism, you were received into the visible Church. Your baptism signified that you had first of all believed on the Lord Jesus Christ and had been regenerated by the power of the Holy Spirit. You now come to take upon yourself the responsibilities, rights and privileges of full membership in this Church, and so to be admitted to participation in The Lord's Supper regularly, but worthily, with the other members of the Household of Faith. I require you not to *re-affirm the vows* you have made through decision and commitment to God in Christ by answering the following questions. Please stand.

Do you reaffirm your faith in the Lord Jesus Christ, and desire from henceforth to be His disciple?

Convert: (Each answers in turn.)

I do.

Minister:

Do you promise to give yourself in holy obedience to the service of God in Christ through this Church and wherever else the opportunity presents itself?

Convert:

I do.

Minister:

Do you promise to be loyal to your Church, faithful in your obligations to the Church, giving honor in all things to God in Christ and not to covet it for yourself?

Convert:

I do.

Minister:

Do you accept the congregational form of government of your Church, and will you be governed by her rules and regulations, insofar as you are able?

Convert:

I do.

Minister:

Do you promise regularly to attend the public services of worship, to support the Church with your substance, to engage in private devotions, and continue to increase your knowledge of the Christian Faith and the administration of your Church?

Convert:

I do.

Minister:

Then I give to you the *Right Hand of Fellowship,* receiving you into full membership of this Church.

Right Hand of Fellowship and Hymn:

The Minister leaves the Pulpit, leading the procession of Ministers and Deacons and the Congregation in extending the Right Hand of Fellowship to the Converts who, in the meantime, have been directed to stand now with their faces toward the Congregation. An appropriate Hymn may be sung during this act. Then shall follow the celebration of The Lord's Supper.

THE LORD'S SUPPER:

The Minister, having taken his place behind the Lord's Table, shall begin the Celebration by saying the following or familiar Sentences from Holy Scriptures and giving a Brief Address.

Sentences:

For God so loved the world, that he gave his only begotten Son, that whosoever believeth in him should not perish, but have everlasting life. — John 3:16.

This is a faithful saying, and worthy of all acceptation, that Christ Jesus came into the world to save sinners; of whom I am chief. — I Timothy 1:15.

Introductory Words:

As we draw near to the Lord's Table, we are gratefully to remember that our Lord instituted this Supper. He is our Host in this House and the Head of this Table. Let us remember that as often as we observe this ordinance we "show forth the Lord's death till he come." We perform this act in remembrance of Him, and to signify our union with Him and our fellowship with those who are members of His Church visible and invisible.

Let us now give thanks to God and seek His blessing in the breaking of bread.

Prayer:

Almighty God, our heavenly Father, who didst give Thy Son to die for the redemption of the world: We thank Thee for Thy great love expressed to us in the gift and sacrifice of our Lord Jesus Christ. We thank Thee for the Church which Thou hast established by the blood of Thine only begotten Son, and for all the means of grace available to us therein. For the fellowship of the saints on earth and in heaven, we humbly thank Thee. Make our communion with them and Thee real and blessed. Grant unto us, we beseech Thee, Thy presence and the power of the Holy Spirit to sanctify these elements which are to be used in this Supper. May we receive Christ more fully into our lives as we observe this Ordinance, and help us to offer our lives to Thee for deeper consecration and a bolder testimony of Thy undying love for us; through Jesus Christ our Lord. Amen.

Distribution of the Bread and Wine:

The elements having been prepared for distribution, the Deacons serving at the Table shall receive them in turn from the hand of the Minister, first the Bread and then the Wine.

The Bread

The Lord Jesus took bread, and when He had blessed it, He broke it, and gave it to His disciples, as I now give this bread to you in His Name *[hands the Bread to the Deacons to distribute]*, saying, Take, eat; this is My body, broken for you; this do in remembrance of Me.

The Wine

After the same manner our Lord took the cup, and, having given thanks, as I have done in His Name, He gave it to His disciples, as I now give it to you *[hands the Wine to the Deacons to distribute]*, saying, This cup is the New Covenant in My blood; drink ye all of it.

HYMN: *(sung after the Lord's Supper has been concluded)*

BENEDICTION:

The God of peace, that brought again from the dead our Lord Jesus, that great Shepherd of the sheep, through the blood of the everlasting covenant, make you perfect in every good work to do his will, working in you that which is well-pleasing in his sight; through Jesus Christ, to whom be glory for ever and ever. Amen.

SERVICE FOR RECOGNITION AND INSTALLATION OF CHURCH OFFICERS AND LEADERS

CALL TO WORSHIP AND INVOCATION

HYMN

PSALM

HYMN OR ANTHEM

NEW TESTAMENT LESSON

ACT OF INSTALLATION

    ADDRESS TO OFFICERS AND LEADERS

    PRAYER

    HYMN

    RIGHT HAND OF FELLOWSHIP

SERMON

OFFERING AND DEDICATION

HYMN

BENEDICTION

When this Act is made a part of a regular Service of Worship, the necessary modifications should be made. The Order presented here is for a special Service.

At the hour appointed for this Service the elected Officers and Leaders should be seated in reserved pews in front of the pulpit. When there are a great many Officers and Leaders to be recognized and inducted into office, a printed list with their names

*and the offices to which they have been elected should be dis-
tributed among the Congregation. Or this information may be
read by someone assigned this task. The hour for the Service
having arrived, the Minister shall give the Call to Worship
with Sentences from Holy Scripture, followed by an Invocation.
The Congregation shall stand through the singing of the first
Hymn.*

CALL TO WORSHIP:

Great is the Lord, and greatly to be praised; and his greatness
is unsearchable.

One generation shall praise thy works to another, and shall
declare thy mighty acts.

I will speak of the glorious honour of thy majesty, and of
thy wondrous works. — Psalm 145:3-5.

INVOCATION:

Almighty God, our heavenly Father, draw our thoughts to Thee
as we worship Thee from this Zion. Open our hearts that Thou
mayest come in, and quiet our spirits that we may hear Thy
voice. We would beseech Thee to bless our coming together,
and open our lips that our mouths may show forth Thy praise;
through Jesus Christ our Lord. Amen.

HYMN: *(a Hymn of praise, such as one of the following)*
   "Come, Thou Almighty King"
   "Mighty God, While Angels Bless Thee"
   "O Could I Speak the Matchless Worth"
   "All Hail the Power of Jesus' Name"

PSALM:

Blessed is the man that walketh not in the counsel of the
ungodly, nor standeth in the way of sinners, nor sitteth in the
seat of the scornful.

But his delight is in the law of the Lord; and in his law doth
he meditate day and night.

And he shall be like a tree planted by the rivers of water,
that bringeth forth his fruit in his season; his leaf also shall
not wither; and whatsoever he doeth shall prosper.

The ungodly are not so: but are like the chaff which the wind driveth away.

Therefore the ungodly shall not stand in the judgment, nor sinners in the congregation of the righteous.

For the Lord knoweth the way of the righteous: but the way of the ungodly shall perish. — Psalm 1.

HYMN OR ANTHEM:

NEW TESTAMENT LESSON:

I therefore, the prisoner of the Lord, beseech you that ye walk worthy of the vocation wherewith ye are called.

With all lowliness and meekness, with long-suffering, forbearing one another in love;

Endeavouring to keep the unity of the Spirit in the bond of peace.

There is one body, and one Spirit, even as ye are called in one hope of your calling;

One Lord, one faith, one baptism,

One God and Father of all, who is above all, and through all, and in you all.

But unto every one of us is given grace according to the measure of the gift of Christ.

Wherefore he saith, When he ascended up on high, he led captivity captive, and gave gifts unto men.

And he gave some, apostles; and some, prophets; and some, evangelists; and some, pastors and teachers;

For the perfecting of the saints, for the work of the ministry, for the edifying of the body of Christ:

Till we all come in the unity of the faith, and of the knowledge of the Son of God, unto a perfect man, unto the measure of the stature of the fulness of Christ. — Ephesians 4:1-8, 11-13.

— or —

Thou therefore, my son, be strong in the grace that is in Christ Jesus.

And the things that thou hast heard of me among many witnesses, the same commit thou to faithful men, who shall be able to teach others also.

Thou therefore endure hardness, as a good soldier of Jesus
Christ.

No man that warreth entangleth himself with the affairs of
this life; that he may please him who hath chosen him to be
a soldier.

And if a man also strive for masteries, yet is he not crowned,
except he strive lawfully.

The husbandman that laboureth must be first partaker of the
fruits.

Consider what I say; and the Lord give thee understanding
in all things. — II Timothy 2:1-7.

ACT OF INSTALLATION:

Address to Officers, Leaders, and Congregation:

*The Minister: (directing the elected Officers and Leaders to
stand)*

For as much as you have been elected by fellow members
of this Church to serve as Officers and Leaders and you have
declared your willingness to serve, I now ask your public
assent to the following questions:

Do you accept the responsibilities of the office into which
you are being installed, and will you, insofar as you can, discharge your duties faithfully and efficiently?

Officers and Leaders: (Each answers in turn.)

I do.

Minister:

Will you seek to promote and maintain a sympathetic and
friendly relationship with those with whom you will be
working so that the bond of fellowship throughout the
Church may be strengthened?

Officers and Leaders:

I will.

Minister:

Do you promise to be faithful to your Church, consistent
in your attendance upon Divine Worship and dutiful in your
support of the total program of your Church?

Officers and Leaders:

I do.

Minister:

Do you promise to honor God and your Church in your service, behavior and conduct?

Officers and Leaders:

I do.

Minister: (to Congregation)

The responsibilities which these Officers and Leaders are now called upon to assume, cannot be discharged by them alone. They have promised, insofar as they are able, to serve their offices well. But their best efforts will fail of fulfillment unless they are supported by the wholehearted and consistent cooperation of all the members of this Church.

Do you, the members of this Congregation, acknowledge and receive these Brothers and Sisters as your duly elected officers? Do you promise to give them the honor, encouragement and cooperation to which their office entitles them? If so, signify the same by standing.

Minister: (to Officers and Leaders)

Then I declare you duly inducted into the office to which you have been elected. May the grace of God be with you, and may you enjoy the confidence and support of your fellow members. Now let us unite our hearts in a Prayer of Consecration.

Prayer:

Almighty and everlasting God, our Father: As we now install these new Officers and Leaders into the offices to which they have been elected, we pray that Thou wilt approve the choices we have made and bless these Thy servants with the outpouring of Thy Holy Spirit. Grant them, O God, a faith as great as the measure of their task, and enrich their lives by full surrender and commitment to Thee. May they see themselves as being committed to a great and divinely large cause so that they may not become discouraged by hindrances or failures of the moment or by difficulties which, in any given moment, they cannot overcome. Grant them, we beseech Thee, the wisdom to know what is vital and essential, what is spiritually indispensable, that they may not waste or dissipate their energies or best effort upon tasks which do not represent the highest. Consecrate them to the work and service to which they have been elected; reinforce their duty with a deep loyalty to Thy cause; lift their work and service to the high plane of a Christian calling; and keep them inspired with Thy everpresent Spirit; through Jesus Christ our Lord. Amen.

Hymn: (a Hymn of consecration, such as one of the following, while the Right Hand of Fellowship is given to the newly installed Officers and Leaders)

"Take My Life and Let It Be"
"O Master, Let Me Walk with Thee"
"I Am Thine, O Lord"
"A Charge to Keep I Have"
"Jesus Keep Me near the Cross"

The Right Hand of Fellowship:

Sermon or Address:

Offering and Dedication:

Hymn: *(congregation standing)*

The Benediction:

The peace of God, which passeth all understanding, keep your hearts and minds in the knowledge and love of God, and of his Son Jesus Christ our Lord: And the blessing of God Almighty, the Father, the Son, and the Holy Ghost, be amongst you, and remain with you always. Amen.

SERVICE FOR ORDINATION OF A DEACON

Opening Sentences and Invocation
Hymn
Scripture Reading
Prayer

HYMN

SERMON

HYMN

ACT OF ORDINATION

    ADDRESS TO THE CANDIDATE AND THE CONGREGATION

    ORDINATION PRAYER AND ORDINATION

    RIGHT HAND OF FELLOWSHIP AND HYMN

The order of procedure having been arranged, the Minister and all others participating in the Ordination enter the Sanctuary at the hour appointed for the Service. The Candidate shall be seated in a place reserved for him in front of the Pulpit. Then shall the Minister say the following or similar Sentences from the Holy Scriptures. The Congregation shall stand through the singing of the first Hymn.

OPENING SENTENCES:

    Blessed is every one that feareth the Lord; that walketh in his ways. — Psalm 128:1.

    Behold, bless ye the Lord, all ye servants of the Lord, which by night stand in the house of the Lord.

    Lift up your hands in the sanctuary, and bless the Lord.

    The Lord that made heaven and earth bless thee out of Zion. — Psalm 134.

INVOCATION: *(in the following or similar words)*

    O gracious God, our heavenly Father, who hast made known to us the exceeding riches of Thy grace: Be pleased to bestow Thy favor upon us assembled in this place, and quicken us by the power of Thy Holy Spirit that we may call upon Thy name in sincerity and truth. Let Thy presence be with us in praise and prayer and in Thy Holy Word; we pray through Jesus Christ our Lord. Amen.

HYMN: *(a Hymn of praise, such as one of the following)*

    "Come, We That Love the Lord"

    "Come, Thou Almighty King"

    "Come, Thou Fount of Every Blessing"

"O Bless the Lord, My Soul"
"O God of Bethel, by Whose Hand"

Scripture Reading:

From the Old Testament

And the Lord said unto Moses, Gather unto me seventy men of the elders of Israel, whom thou knowest to be the elders of the people, and officers over them; and bring them unto the tabernacle of the congregation, that they may stand there with thee.

And I will come down and talk with thee there: and I will take of the spirit which is upon thee, and will put it upon them; and they shall bear the burden of the people with thee, that thou bear it not thyself alone.

And Moses went out, and told the people the words of the Lord, and gathered the seventy men of the elders of the people, and set them round about the tabernacle.

And the Lord came down in a cloud, and spake unto him, and took of the spirit that was upon him, and gave it unto the seventy elders: and it came to pass, that, when the spirit rested upon them, they prophesied, and did not cease.

But there remained two of the men in the camp, the name of the one was Eldad, and the name of the other Medad: and the spirit rested upon them; and they were of them that were written, but went not out unto the tabernacle: and they prophesied in the camp.

And there ran a young man, and told Moses, and said, Eldad and Medad do prophesy in the camp.

And Joshua the son of Nun, the servant of Moses, one of his young men, answered and said, My lord Moses, forbid them.

And Moses said unto him, Enviest thou for my sake? would God that all the Lord's people were prophets, and that the Lord would put his spirit upon them! — Numbers 11:16-17, 24-29.

From the New Testament

Whosoever will be great among you, let him be your minister;
And whosoever will be chief among you, let him be your servant:

Even as the Son of man came not to be ministered unto, but to minister, and to give his life a ransom for many. — Matthew 20:26-28.

— or —

Likewise must the deacons be grave, not doubletongued, not given to much wine, not greedy of filthy lucre;

Holding the mystery of the faith in a pure conscience.

And let these also first be proved; then let them use the office of a deacon, being found blameless.

Even so must their wives be grave, not slanderers, sober, faithful in all things.

Let the deacons be the husbands of one wife, ruling their children and their own houses well.

For they that have used the office of a deacon well purchase to themselves a good degree, and great boldness in the faith which is in Christ Jesus. — I Timothy 3:8-13.

PRAYER: *(in which aspirations of the Candidates are set forth in the following or similar words)*

Almighty God, and Father of our Lord and Saviour Jesus Christ, enlighten our minds that we may understand Thy Holy Word. Open all the windows of our souls so that the fullness of Thy light and wisdom may come in. Touch our hearts with Thy grace that we may receive Thy counsels with all reverence, humility and obedience. Grant that Thy Word may be a lamp unto our feet and a light unto our path. Teach us, through Thy Holy Word, to trust Thee in all things, and for all things. And since it hath pleased Thee to allow us to be chosen for special service in Thy House, grant that we may offer to Thee the love and obedience, discipline and sacrifice our service demands of us; through Jesus Christ our Lord. Amen.

HYMN: *(a Hymn of aspiration, such as one of the following, the congregation standing)*

"I Am Thine, O Lord"
"O for a Closer Walk with God"
"Jesus Keep Me near the Cross"
"I'm Pressing on the Upward Way"

SERMON: *(in which the duties, privileges, and personal demands of the Office of Deacon may be stressed)*

HYMN: *(a Hymn of faith or courage such as one of the following, the congregation standing)*

"My Soul, Be on Thy Guard"
"Must Jesus Bear the Cross Alone"
"A Charge to Keep I Have"
"Am I a Soldier of the Cross?"

ACT OF ORDINATION:

Address to the Candidate and the Congregation

Minister: (to the Candidate, who is directed to stand)

Do you believe that the Scriptures of the Old and New Testaments are the Word of God, and that they are the only rule of faith and practice of the Church?

Candidate:

I do so believe.

Minister:

Will you heed the Scripture which says: Sanctify the Lord God in your hearts: and be ready always to give an answer to every man that asketh you a reason of the hope that is in you with meekness and fear? — I Peter 3:15.

Candidate:

I will.

Minister:

Do you promise to assist your Minister as a faithful helper, and endeavor to preserve peace and harmony within the fellowship?

Candidate:

I promise so to do.

Minister:

Do you approve of the form of government of your Church; and are you persuaded that the Church alone has authoritative control over the regulation of its own affairs?

Candidate:

I do.

Minister:

Do you now, in the presence of this Congregation, accept your selection to the Office of Deacon in this Church, and solemnly promise to the best of your knowledge and ability, to discharge all the duties of this office?

Candidate:

I do.

Minister: (to the Congregation)

Do you, members of this Congregation, acknowledge and receive *this Brother* as a Deacon; and do you solemnly promise to respect and honor the office to which he has been chosen, encouraging and supporting him in the faithful discharge of all the duties of this office? If so, signify the same by rising and joining your hearts with ours in the Prayer of Ordination.

The people rising, the Minister leaves the pulpit and takes his place in front of the pulpit on the floor level or in the chancel, as the case may be. The Candidate is directed to kneel in front of the Minister. The Minister and Deacons associated with him lay their hands on the Candidate's head as the Ordination Prayer is given.

Ordination Prayer and Ordination:

Most gracious and everlasting God, our heavenly Father, who in Thy wisdom hast endowed Thy servants with a diversity of gifts and abilities, but dost call upon us to use them in Thy service: We thank Thee for *this Thy servant* whom we now ordain to the Office of Deacon. Bless *him* with Thy grace, O God, that he may serve honorably and faithfully as a servant in Thy house. Send Thy Holy Spirit upon *him* that his mind may be enlightened and his spirit kindled with Thy holy fire. Make *him* to be wise and diligent in the performance of the temporal affairs of the Church. Teach him how effectively to promote peace, hospitality of spirit and liberality among the members of this Congregation. May he gain a good standing in Thy Church and great boldness in the faith to serve Thee and to do Thy holy will; through Jesus Christ our Lord, who taught us when we pray to say:

Our Father who art in heaven, Hallowed be thy name. Thy Kingdom come. Thy will be done on earth, as it is in heaven. Give us this day our daily bread. And forgive us our debts, as we forgive our debtors. And lead us not into temptation; But deliver us from evil: For thine is the kingdom, and the power, and the glory, for ever. Amen.

The Ordination Prayer being ended, and the Candidate having risen, the Minister shall say:

By the authority given unto me by our Lord Jesus Christ, and by the authority of this Church, I now declare you to be ordained to the Office of Deacon in this Church. May God bless you and may His Spirit be with you always. I now give you the Right Hand of Fellowship in token of your acceptance by the Congregation.

Right Hand of Fellowship Hymn:

The Minister shall now give his hand to the newly ordained Deacon, and he is followed in this by all the Ministers and Deacons present, as a Hymn of fellowship or consecration, such as one of the following, is being sung. (The Service concludes with the Benediction, the congregation standing.)

"Leaning on the Everlasting Arms"
"Blest Be the Tie That Binds"
"I Can Hear My Saviour Calling"
"Is Your All on the Altar?"
"We're Marching to Zion"
"I Love Thy Kingdom, Lord"

BENEDICTION:

The grace of the Lord Jesus Christ, the love of God the Father, and the communion of the Holy Spirit, be with you all for ever Amen.

SERVICE FOR LICENSING A PERSON TO PREACH

Opening Sentences

Hymn

Prayer

Scripture Readings From the Old and New Testaments

Hymn

Act of Licensing

    Address to the Licentiate

    Licensing

    Presentation of Bible

    Prayer

Hymn

Benediction

This Act may be a part of a regular Sunday Morning Worship Service, or it may be performed at a special Service arranged specifically for this purpose. When a part of a regular Sunday Morning Worship Service, this Order should be abbreviated.

At the appointed hour for this Service the Licentiate shall be seated in the Church in a place reserved for him in front of the Minister. The Minister shall say one or more Sentences from Holy Scripture. The Congregation shall stand through the singing of the first Hymn.

Opening Sentences:

[Hear the words of our Lord as He spoke to His disciples in Galilee:] All power is given unto me in heaven and in earth. . . . Go ye into all the world, and preach the gospel to every creature.

He that believeth and is baptized shall be saved; but he that believeth not shall be damned. — Matthew 28:18; Mark 16:15-16.

[Hear also the words of the apostle Paul:] For though I preach the gospel, I have nothing to glory of: for necessity is laid upon me; yea, woe is unto me, if I preach not the gospel!

For we preach not ourselves, but Christ Jesus the Lord . . . .

But we have this treasure in earthen vessels, that the excellency of the power may be of God, and not of us. — I Corinthians 9:16; II Corinthians 4:5, 7.

HYMN: *(a Hymn of praise, such as one of the following)*
"All Hail the Power of Jesus' Name"
"How Sweet the Name of Jesus Sounds"
"Rejoice, the Lord Is King"
"O for a Thousand Tongues to Sing"

PRAYER:

Almighty God, our heavenly Father, by whose Son the Ministry of the Word has been established and by whose great love we have a Gospel to preach: We thank Thee that thou dost still call into this service redeemed and dedicated men who are willing and ready to answer Thy call and to place upon themselves the burden of a messenger of the Good News. Be Thou with us, O gracious God, in this act of sending our brother forth to preach Thy Word of Life to every creature. For without Thy presence to bless our coming together, we cannot exalt Thy holy Name or be inspired by what we do here. Vouchsafe to us the grace of Thy presence; through Jesus Christ our Lord. Amen.

SCRIPTURE READING:

From the Old Testament

Comfort ye, comfort ye my people, saith your God.

Speak ye comfortably to Jerusalem, and cry unto her, that her warfare is accomplished, that her iniquity is pardoned: for she hath received of the Lord's hand double for all her sins.

The voice of him that crieth in the wilderness, Prepare ye the way of the Lord, make straight in the desert a highway for our God.

Every valley shall be exalted, and every mountain and hill shall be made low: and the crooked shall be made straight, and the rough places plain:

All the glory of the Lord shall be revealed, and all flesh shall see it together: for the mouth of the Lord hath spoken it.

16913

The voice said, Cry. And he said, What shall I cry? All flesh is grass, and all the goodliness thereof is as the flower of the field:

The grass withereth, the flower fadeth: because the spirit of the Lord bloweth upon it: surely the people is grass.

The grass withereth, the flower fadeth: but the word of our God shall stand for ever.

O Zion, that bringest good tidings, get thee up into the high mountain; O Jerusalem, that bringest good tidings, lift up thy voice with strength; lift it up, be not afraid; say unto the cities of Judah, Behold your God!

Behold, the Lord God will come with strong hand, and his arm shall rule for him: behold, his reward is with him, and his work before him.

He shall feed his flock like a shepherd: he shall gather the lambs with his arm, and carry them in his bosom, and shall gently lead those that are with young. — Isaiah 40:1-11.

From the New Testament

For the preaching of the cross is to them that perish foolishness; but unto us which are saved it is the power of God.

For ye see your calling, brethren, how that not many wise men after the flesh, not many mighty, not many noble, are called:

But God hath chosen the foolish things of the world to confound the wise; and God hath chosen the weak things of the world to confound the things which are mighty;

And base things of the world, and things which are despised, hath God chosen, yea, and things which are not, to bring to nought things that are:

That no flesh should glory in his presence.

But of him are ye in Christ Jesus, who of God is made into us wisdom, and righteousness, and sanctification, and redemption:

That, according as it is written, He that glorieth, let him glory in the Lord. — I Corinthians 1:18, 26-37.

— *or* —

I charge thee therefore before God, and the Lord Jesus Christ, who shall judge the quick and the dead at his appearing and his kingdom;

Preach the word; be instant in season, out of season; reprove, rebuke, exhort with all long suffering and doctrine.

For the time will come when they will not endure sound doctrine; but after their own lusts shall they heap to themselves teachers, having itching ears;

And they shall turn away their ears from the truth, and shall be turned unto fables.

But watch thou in all things, endure afflictions, do the work of an evangelist, make full proof of thy ministry. — II Timothy 4:1-5.

HYMN: *(a Hymn of the Holy Spirit, such as one of the following, the congregation standing)*

"Come, Holy Spirit, Heavenly Dove"
"Holy Spirit, Truth Divine"
"Spirit Divine Attend Our Prayer"
"Spirit of God, Descend upon My Heart"

ACT OF LICENSING:

Address to the Congregation:

Brothers and Sisters in Christ, we have gathered together here today publicly to acknowledge N.'s call to the Gospel Ministry and to give him such authorization as is required to preach the Gospel as a representative of Christ and this Church. His period of trial has now terminated and you, being convinced of his call and pleased with his performance, have approved the recommendation coming from the Pastor and the Board of Deacons that he be granted a license to preach.

Address to the Licentiate:

N., will you now stand. *(Pause while Licentiate stands.)* Insofar as you know your own heart, do you believe that you have received a divine call to the Gospel Ministry?

Licentiate:

I do.

Minister:

Do you believe the Scriptures of the Old and New Testaments to be the Word of God, that they are the only rule of our faith and practice, and that the Gospel of Christ is the power of God unto salvation to every one that believeth?

Licentiate:

I do so believe.

Minister:

Do you solemnly promise to show yourself approved unto God, a workman that needeth not to be ashamed, rightly dividing the word of truth?

Licentiate:

I do.

Minister:

Then, in the name of the Lord Jesus Christ, the Head of the Church, the Ground and Pillar of Truth, and by the authority which He has given His Church, you are hereby licensed to preach the Gospel wherever God in His Providence may call you. We send you forth in the name of Christ, and may the blessings of the Father rest upon you. May His Son inspire you; and may the Holy Spirit empower and embolden you. Amen.

Presentation of Bible:

(The Minister now hands the Licentiate a Bible.)

Take now this Bible, of which you are appointed an interpreter. Be diligent to study the truths written therein. Take them into your own heart so that they may be imparted to others with warmth, conviction and power. And to the extent of your understanding and ability, faithfully and truthfully preach the Gospel of the grace of God. Be yourself an example of faith and devoted living under God in Christ so that no one, in following you, may stumble or fall or be lost to the Kingdom of God and the Church.

Prayer:

O eternal God, our Father, who from the beginning didst choose men to be the carriers of Thy Holy Word, Thou who hast sent them out into the world as apostles, evangelists, pastors and teachers: We beseech Thee to grant Thy gifts of grace and power, of prophetic zeal and apostolic fire, to this Thy servant that, through him, Thy Word may be effectively and faithfully preached, Thy name magnified, and many souls brought to Thee; we ask this through Jesus Christ our Lord. Amen.

HYMN: *(one of the following, the congregation standing to the conclusion of the Service)*

"Go Preach My Gospel, Saith the Lord"
"I'll Go Where You Want Me to Go"
"Beneath the Cross of Jesus"
"Lord, Speak to Me, that I May Speak"
"I Love to Tell the Story"

BENEDICTION:

The grace of the Lord Jesus Christ, and the love of God, and the communion of the Holy Spirit, be with you all. Amen.

SERVICE FOR ORDINATION OF A MINISTER

CALL TO WORSHIP AND INVOCATION
HYMN
SCRIPTURE READINGS FROM THE OLD AND NEW TESTAMENTS
PRAYER
HYMN
SERMON
ACT OF ORDINATION
    ADDRESS TO THE ORDINAND

ORDINATION PRAYER AND ORDINATION
RIGHT HAND OF FELLOWSHIP AND HYMN
CHARGE TO THE ORDAINED AND THE CONGREGATION
HYMN
PRAYER
BENEDICTION

The order of procedure having been arranged, the Presiding Minister and all Ministers participating in the Ordination shall enter the Sanctuary at the hour of service. The Ordinand shall be seated in a place reserved for him in front of the Pulpit, and should be joined by his wife, if married. The Presiding Minister shall give the Call to Worship, following this with an Invocation. The Congregation shall stand through the singing of the first Hymn.

CALL TO WORSHIP

Praise waiteth for thee, O God, in Zion: and unto thee shall the vow be performed.

Blessed is the man whom thou choosest, and causest to approach unto thee, that he may dwell in thy courts: we shall be satisfied with the goodness of thy house, even of thy holy temple. — Psalm 65:1, 4.

This is a true saying, If a man desire the office of a bishop, he desireth a good work. — I Timothy 3:1.

INVOCATION:

Almighty and everlasting God, who brought salvation and good news to the world through Thy Son Jesus Christ and who hast, through Thy Son, commanded us to preach and to teach, baptizing the believer in the name of the Father, and of the Son, and of the Holy Spirit: Grant to us Thy presence now that what we do in this hour may be done to Thy honor and to Thy glory. Give us hearts and minds that are sensitive to Thy presence and hospitable to Thy Spirit as we perform the act that has brought us together here; we pray through Jesus Christ our Lord. Amen.

HYMN: *(a Hymn of praise, such as one of the following)*
> "Come, Ye That Know and Fear the Lord"
> "Begin, My Tongue, Some Heavenly Theme"
> "O for a Thousand Tongues to Sing"
> "How Sweet the Name of Jesus Sounds"
> "Come, Thou Fount of Every Blessing"
> "What Equal Honors Shall We Bring"

SCRIPTURE READING:

From the Old Testament

In the year that king Uzziah died I saw also the Lord sitting upon a throne, high and lifted up, and his train filled the temple.

Above it stood the seraphims: each one had six wings; with twain he covered his face, and with twain he covered his feet, and with twain he did fly.

And one cried unto another, and said, Holy, holy, holy, is the Lord of hosts: the whole earth is full of his glory.

And the posts of the door moved at the voice of him that cried, and the house was filled with smoke.

Then said I, Woe is me! for I am undone; because I am a man of unclean lips, and I dwell in the midst of a people of unclean lips: for mine eyes have seen the King, the Lord of hosts.

Then flew one of the seraphims unto me, having a live coal in his hand, which he had taken with the tongs from off the altar:

And he laid it upon my mouth, and said, Lo, this hath touched thy lips; and thine iniquity is taken away, and thy sin purged.

Also I heard the voice of the Lord, saying, Whom shall I send, and who will go for us? Then said I, Here am I; send me. — Isaiah 6:1-8.

— *or* —

Again the word of the Lord came unto me, saying,

Son of man, speak to the children of thy people, and say unto them, When I bring the sword upon a land, if the people of the land take a man of their coasts, and set him for their watchman:

If when he seeth the sword come upon the land, he blow the trumpet, and warn the people;

Then whosoever heareth the sound of the trumpet, and taketh not warning; if the sword come, and take him away, his blood shall be upon his own head.

He heard the sound of the trumpet, and took not warning; his blood shall be upon him. But he that taketh warning shall deliver his soul.

But if the watchman see the sword come, and blow not the trumpet, and the people be not warned; if the sword come, and take any person from among them, he is taken away in his iniquity; but his blood will I require at the watchman's hand.

So thou, O son of man, I have set thee a watchman unto the house of Israel; therefore thou shalt hear the word at my mouth, and warn them from me.

When I say unto the wicked, O wicked man, thou shalt surely die; if thou dost not speak to warn the wicked from his way, that wicked man shall die in his iniquity; but his blood will I require at thine hand.

Nevertheless, if thou warn the wicked of his way to turn from it; if he do not turn from his way, he shall die in his iniquity; but thou hast delivered thy soul. — Ezekiel 33:1-9.

From the New Testament

And it came to pass, that, as they went in the way a certain man said unto him, Lord, I will follow thee whithersoever thou goest.

And Jesus said unto him, Foxes have holes, and birds of the air have nests; but the Son of man hath not where to lay his head.

And he said unto another, Follow me. But he said, Lord, suffer me first to go and bury my father.

Jesus said unto him, Let the dead bury their dead: but go thou and preach the kingdom of God.

And another also said, Lord, I will follow thee; but let me first go bid them farewell, which are at home at my house.

And Jesus said unto him, No man, having put his hand to the plow and looking back, is fit for the kingdom of God. — Luke 9:57-62.

— *or* —

If thou put the brethren in remembrance of these things, thou shalt be a good minister of Jesus Christ, nourished up in the words of faith and of good doctrine, whereunto thou hast attained.

But refuse profane and old wives' fables, and exercise thyself rather unto godliness.

For bodily exercise profiteth little: but godliness is profitable unto all things, having promise of the life that now is, and of that which is to come.

This is a faithful saying and worthy of all acceptation.

For therefore we both labour and suffer reproach, because we trust in the living God, who is the Saviour of all men, specially of those that believe.

These things command and teach.

Let no man despise thy youth; but be thou an example of the believers, in word, in conversation, in charity, in spirit, in faith, in purity.

Till I come, give attendance to reading, to exhortation, to doctrine.

Neglect not the gift that is in thee, which was given thee by prophecy, with the laying on of the hands of the presbytery.

Meditate upon these things; give thyself wholly to them; that thy profiting may appear to all.

Take heed unto thyself, and unto the doctrine; continue in them: for in doing this thou shalt both save thyself, and them that hear thee. — I Timothy 4:6-16.

PRAYER: *(a Prayer for illumination and receptivity of divine guidance)*
Almighty God, and Father of our Lord and Saviour Jesus Christ: Enlighten our minds that we may understand Thy Holy Word. Open all the windows of our souls that the fullness of Thy light and wisdom may come in. Touch our hearts with Thy grace that we may receive Thy counsels with all reverence,

humility and obedience. Grant that Thy Word may be a lamp unto our feet and a light unto our path. Teach us, through Thy Holy Word, to trust Thee in all things, and for all things. And since it hath pleased Thee to allow us, Thy servants, to be entrusted with the Gospel, grant that we may offer to Thee the love and obedience, discipline and sacrifice, our calling demands of us; through Jesus Christ our Lord. Amen.

HYMN: (a Hymn of courage or faith, such as one of the following, the Congregation standing)

"Must Jesus Bear the Cross Alone"
"Are Ye Able, Said the Master"
"My Soul, Be on Thy Guard"
"Stand Up, Stand Up for Jesus"

SERMON: (followed by Questions to the Ordinand, who is directed to stand)

ACT OF ORDINATION:

Address to the Ordinand:

Minister:

Do you promise to walk worthy of the vocation to which you are called, giving honor to God who, of His mercy, has called you to be a shepherd of His flock?

Ordinand:

I do.

Minister:

Do you promise faithfully and diligently to perform all the duties of a faithful Minister of the Gospel without thought of personal reward or honor, having as your chief motives the honor of God, the exaltation of Christ, the winning and Christian growth of souls and the glory of Christ's Church?

Ordinand:

I do.

Minister:

Then kneel for the Prayer of Ordination and the laying on of hands.

The Presiding Minister shall then leave the Pulpit and take his place in front of the Pulpit on the floor level or in the Chancel, as the case may be. The Ordinand is directed to kneel in front of the Presiding Minister. The Presiding Minister and the Ministers associated with him lay their hands on the Ordinand's head as the Ordination Prayer is given.

Ordination Prayer and Ordination:

Almighty God, our heavenly Father, who brought again from the dead our Lord Jesus Christ, and, who for the salvation, communion and edification of Thy people, didst establish the Church: We pray for this our brother who is now being set apart to the high office of the Christian ministry of the Word and the administration of the Ordinances of the Church. Teach him the true and solemn meaning of this act, the vows he is taking, and the demands and responsibilities he is accepting through this act. May he be truly set apart for this service into which he is called and is now being granted its rights and privileges. Help him to know, O gracious God, that from this day there is no turning from the choice he has made and the way he has chosen. To follow and never to look back, to place his hands to the Gospel plough and never let go, is the cost of his decision and consecration to the office of the Holy Ministry. Be Thou with him, O merciful Father, to strengthen him when he is weak; to guide him when his way is not clear; to cheer him when he is saddened and discouraged; to reassure him when doubts arise; and to company with him when he is lonely. Let Thy Holy Spirit, we beseech Thee, fit him for all the work of this Ministry and correct him in wilful or ignorant mistakes. May he be a faithful and loving shepherd of Thy sheep, and may he not neglect to care for Thy lambs. May he be among those who win many souls to Thee and bring comfort, guidance and knowledge to the saved. Make him helpful to his yokefellows in the Ministry and give him a great love for Thy Church. Be with us now, O merciful Father, as in the name of Thy Son Jesus Christ, and by the authority of this Church, we ordain this Thy servant to the office of the Christian Ministry with the laying on of hands. May he be filled with the Holy Spirit and power from on high. And when his service is ended here, may he hear Thy voice saying unto him: "Well done, thou good and faithful servant"; we pray through Jesus Christ our Lord, who taught us when we pray to say:

Our Father which art in heaven, Hallowed by thy name. Thy kingdom come. Thy will be done on earth, as it is in heaven. Give us this day our daily bread. And forgive us our debts, as we forgive our debtors. And lead us not into temptation, but deliver us from evil: For thine is the kingdom, and the power, and the glory, for ever. Amen.

The Ordination Prayer being ended and the Ordinand having risen, the Presiding Minister shall say:

By the authority given unto me by our Lord Jesus Christ, the Head and Chief Cornerstone of the Church, and by the authority of this Church, I now declare you to be ordained to the office of the Christian Ministry. May God bless you and may His Spirit be with you always. I now give you the Right Hand of Fellowship in token of your acceptance into the fellowship of the Gospel.

Right Hand of Fellowship and Hymn:

The Presiding Minister shall then give his hand to the Ordinand, and shall be followed in this by all the Ministers associated with him, as a Hymn of the Holy Spirit, such as one of the following, is being sung. The Congregation shall stand.

"Gracious Spirit, Dwell with Me"
"Come, Holy Spirit, Heavenly Dove"
"Spirit of the Living God"
"Spirit Divine, Attend Our Prayer"
"Holy Spirit, Faithful Guide"
"Breathe on Me, Breath of God"

Charge to the Ordained and the Congregation:

Here may follow the Charges to the Ordained and the Congregation. The Ordained shall stand when being addressed by the Minister appointed to give him the Charge, the Charge being reasonably short. The Congregation need not stand to receive the Charge addressed to it by the Minister appointed for this, although this Charge should be reasonably short.

HYMN: *(a closing Hymn such as one of the following, the Congregation standing)*

"The Lord Is My Shepherd"
"Great Is Thy Faithfulness"
"All the Way My Saviour Leads Me"
"Jesus, Keep Me near the Cross"
"Thou My Everlasting Portion"
"O Master, Let Me Walk with Thee"

PRAYER: *(the Congregation seated for this and the Benediction)*
All wise and everlasting God, our heavenly Father: We thank Thee for this our brother who, through his labor and faithfulness to this Church, has already witnessed effectively to the power of a holy affection. Continue Thou with him, O Lord, as he shall leave the care and guidance of this Church. And what we have failed to give or be to him, do Thou supply for him, O God, that he may be adequate for the task that is set before him and an honor to Thee and to the Church from which he shall go forth. May Thy Church always be instrumental not only in the conversion of souls to Thee but in inspiring and leading men to desire and to accept the high calling of the Christian Ministry; through Jesus Christ our Lord. Amen.

BENEDICTION:
Now the God of Peace, that brought again from the dead our Lord Jesus, that great shepherd of the sheep, through the blood of his everlasting covenant, make you perfect in every good work to do his will, working in you that which is well-pleasing in his sight, through Jesus Christ: to whom be glory for ever and ever. Amen.

SERVICE FOR INSTALLATION OF A MINISTER

CALL TO WORSHIP AND INVOCATION

HYMN

OLD TESTAMENT LESSON

HYMN OR ANTHEM
NEW TESTAMENT LESSON
HYMN
WELCOMING REMARKS
HYMN OR ANTHEM
ACT OF INDUCTION
   CHARGE TO THE MINISTER
   CHARGE TO THE CONGREGATION
   INSTALLATION PRAYER
HYMN
SERMON
OFFERING AND DEDICATION
INDUCTED MINISTER'S REMARKS
HYMN
BENEDICTION

It would be well for a newly called Minister to a Church in the community to enlist the counsel and assistance of Ministers well established in their churches and community when preparing for his installation ceremonies. He should certainly seek the guidance and cooperation of any Association of Churches of his denomination and any local Council of Churches as well as the sister churches of the community in which his charge will be located.

It shall not be improvident for him to invite representatives of other community-serving organizations to share in his installation since, in his Ministry, he will need a knowledge of and working relationship with all the resources of the community.

When all procedures have been arranged for this Service, the Minister to be installed having taken a seat in front of the Pulpit with his wife at his side, the Presiding Minister and other officiants shall enter the Sanctuary to begin the Service. The Presiding Minister shall give the Call to Worship, following this with an Invocation. The Congregation shall stand through the singing of the first Hymn.

CALL TO WORSHIP:

Praise waiteth for thee, O God, in Zion: and unto thee shall the vow be performed. O thou that hearest prayer, unto thee shall all flesh come.

Blessed is the man whom thou choosest, and causest to approach unto thee, that he may dwell in thy courts: we shall be satisfied with the goodness of thy house, even of thy holy temple. — Psalm 65: 1-2, 4.

How beautiful upon the mountains are the feet of him that bringeth good tidings, that publisheth peace. — Isaiah 52:7.

INVOCATION:

Almighty and everblessed God, our heavenly Father, who, through Thy Son, hath established for our sake the Church, and without whose Holy Spirit no one can worship Thee acceptably: Grant us Thy grace, we beseech Thee, that we may worship Thee in spirit and in truth. Let what we do here be acceptable to Thee and be done to Thy glory and the edifying of the Body of Christ, the Church; through Jesus Christ our Lord. Amen.

HYMN: (*Hymn of praise, such as one of the following*)

"Ancient of Days, Who Sittest Throned in Glory"
"All Hail the Power of Jesus' Name"
"O for a Thousand Tongues to Sing"

OLD TESTAMENT LESSON:

And he said unto me, Son of man, go, get thee unto the house of Israel, and speak with my words unto them.

For thou art not sent to a people of a strange speech and of hard language, but to the house of Israel;

Not to many people of a strange speech and of hard language, whose words thou canst not understand. Surely, had I sent thee to them, they would have hearkened unto thee.

But the house of Israel will not hearken unto thee; for they will not hearken unto me: for all the house of Israel are impudent and hardhearted.

Behold, I have made thy face strong against their faces, and thy forehead strong against their foreheads.

As an adamant harder than flint have I made thy forehead:

fear them not, neither be dismayed at their looks, though they be a rebellious house.

Moreover he said unto me, Son of man, all my words that I shall speak unto thee receive in thine heart, and hear with thine ears.

And go, get thee to them of the captivity, unto the children of thy people, and speak unto them, and tell them, Thus saith the Lord God; whether they will hear, or whether they will forbear.

Then the spirit took me up, and I heard behind me a voice of a great rushing, saying, Blessed be the glory of the Lord from his place. — Ezekiel 3:4-12.

— *or* —

And the word of the Lord came unto me, saying,

Son of man, prophesy against the shepherds of Israel, prophesy, and say unto them, Thus saith the Lord God unto the shepherds; woe be to the shepherds of Israel that do feed themselves! should not the shepherds feed the flocks?

Ye eat the fat, and ye clothe you with the wool, ye kill them that are fed: but ye feed not the flock.

The diseased have ye not strengthened, neither have ye healed that which was sick, neither have ye bound up that which was broken, neither have ye brought again that which was driven away, neither have ye sought that which was lost; but with force and with cruelty have ye ruled them.

And they were scattered, because there is no shepherd: and they became meat to all the beasts of the field, when they were scattered.

My sheep wandered through all the mountains, and upon every high hill: yea, my flock was scattered upon all the face of the earth, and none did search or seek after them.

Therefore, ye shepherds, hear the word of the Lord;

As I live, saith the Lord God, surely because my flock became a prey, and my flock became meat to every beast of the field, because there was no shepherd, neither did my shepherds search for my flock, but the shepherds fed themselves, and fed not my flock;

Therefore, O ye shepherds, hear the word of the Lord;

Thus saith the Lord God; Behold, I am against the shepherds; and I will require my flock at their hand, and cause them to cease from feeding the flock; neither shall the shepherds feed themselves any more; for I will deliver my flock from their mouth, that they may not be meat for them.

For thus saith the Lord God; Behold, I, even I, will both search my sheep, and seek them out.

As a shepherd seeketh out his flock in the day that he is among his sheep that are scattered; so will I seek out my sheep, and will deliver them out of all places where they have been scattered in the cloudy and dark day. — Ezekiel 34:1-12.

HYMN OR ANTHEM: *(a Hymn of the Holy Spirit or an Anthem)*

NEW TESTAMENT LESSON:

Verily, verily, I say unto you, He that entereth not by the door into the sheepfold, but climbeth up some other way, the same is a thief and a robber.

But he that entereth in by the door is the shepherd of the sheep.

To him the porter openeth; and the sheep hear his voice: and he calleth his own sheep by name, and leadeth them out.

And when he putteth forth his own sheep, he goeth before them, and the sheep follow him; for they know his voice.

And a stranger will they not follow, but will flee from him: for they know not the voice of strangers.

This parable spake Jesus unto them: but they understood not what things they were which he spake unto them.

Then said Jesus unto them again, Verily, verily, I say unto you, I am the door of the sheep.

All that ever came before me are thieves and robbers: but the sheep did not hear them.

I am the door: by me if any man enter in, he shall be saved, and shall go in and out, and find pasture.

The thief cometh not, but for to steal, and to kill, and to destroy: I am come that they might have life, and that they might have it more abundantly.

I am the good shepherd: the good shepherd giveth his life for the sheep.

But he that is an hireling, and not the shepherd, whose own the sheep are not, seeth the wolf coming, and leaveth the sheep, and fleeth: and the wolf catcheth them, and scattereth the sheep.

The hireling fleeth, because he is an hireling, and careth not for the sheep.

I am the good shepherd, and know my sheep, and am known of mine.

As the Father knoweth me, even so know I the Father: and I lay down my life for the sheep.

And other sheep I have, which are not of this fold: them also I must bring, and they shall hear my voice; and there shall be one fold, and one shepherd. — John 10:1-16.

— *or* —

But thou, O man of God, flee these things; and follow after righteousness, godliness, faith, love, patience, meekness.

Fight the good fight of faith, lay hold on eternal life, whereunto thou art also called, and hast professed a good profession before many witnesses.

I give thee charge in the sight of God, who quickeneth all things, and before Christ Jesus, who before Pontius Pilate witnessed a good confession;

That thou keep this commandment without spot, unrebukeable, until the appearing of our Lord Jesus Christ:

Which in his times he shall show, who is the blessed and only Potentate, the King of kings, and Lord of lords;

Who only hath immortality, dwelling in the light which no man can approach unto; whom no man hath seen, nor can see: to whom be honour and power everlasting. Amen.

Charge them that are rich in this world, that they be not high-minded, nor trust in uncertain riches, but in the living God, who giveth us richly all things to enjoy;

That they do good, that they be rich in good works, ready to distribute, willing to communicate;

Laying up in store for themselves a good foundation against

the time to come, that they may lay hold on eternal life. — I Timothy 6:11-19.

— *or* —

The elders which are among you I exhort, who am also an elder, and a witness of the sufferings of Christ, and also a partaker of the glory that shall be revealed:

Feed the flock of God which is among you, taking the oversight thereof, not by constraint, but willingly; not for filthy lucre, but of a ready mind;

Neither as being lords over God's heritage, but being examples to the flock.

And when the chief Shepherd shall appear, ye shall receive a crown of glory that fadeth not away.

Likewise, ye younger, submit yourselves unto the elder. Yea, all of you be subject one to another, and be clothed with humility: for God resisteth the proud, and giveth grace to the humble.

Humble yourselves therefore under the mighty hand of God, that he may exalt you in due time:

Casting all your care upon him, for he careth for you.

Be sober, be vigilant; because your adversary the devil, as a roaring lion, walketh about, seeking whom he may devour:

Whom resist stedfast in the faith, knowing that the same afflictions are accomplished in your brethren that are in the world.

But the God of all grace, who hath called us unto his eternal glory by Christ Jesus, after that ye have suffered a while, make you perfect, stablish, strengthen, settle you.

To him be glory and dominion for ever and ever. Amen. — I Peter 5:1-11.

HYMN: *(a Hymn of the Gospel, such as one of the following, the congregation standing)*

    "We Have Heard the Joyful Sound"
    "I Heard the Voice of Jesus Say"
    "Jesus, Thou Joy of Loving Hearts"
    "Immortal Love, Forever Full"

WELCOMING REMARKS:

Here shall follow brief words of welcome by representatives from the various community-serving organizations, a representative of the Churches of the same denomination in the community, a representative of the Churches of other denominations, the Association of Churches of the Minister's denomination, and a representative of the local Council of Churches.

HYMN OR ANTHEM:

ACT OF INDUCTION:

Charge to the Minister:

Charge to the Congregation:

Installation Prayer:

Almighty and everlasting God, our heavenly Father, who in Thy wisdom hast set over the Household of Faith wise and faithful stewards for the ministry of Thy Word, the administration of Thy Ordinances, the winning of souls, the edification of believers, and for the comfort and counsel of Thy children: Enable this Minister and people, we beseech Thee, to fulfill the duties incumbent upon them in their respective capacities. Give them the grace faithfully to keep the mutual covenant entered into, and may this public confirmation of the promises they have made be approved and sealed by Thy Holy Spirit.

We publicly and sorrowfully acknowledge our human weaknesses, our proneness to error and sin. We admit that at times we are lacking in inner discipline, sound judgment and Christian sympathy and love. But we would plead, O blessed God, for Thy Spirit to strengthen us and Thy love to restrain us when we would dishonor Thee by improper and un-Christian conduct in Thy House or towards each other.

We pray for this Thy servant whom we now induct into office as Minister of this congregation. Be Thou with him in his service here. Be his strength in weakness, his wisdom when important decisions must be made, his courage when circumstances compel him to act uncompromisingly, and his companion when lonely and discouraged. Give him a passion for souls that he may seek the salvation of the lost, comfort those who mourn, minister to the sick and the dying, help the poor and encourage the downhearted. Grant unto him grace to preach the Gospel with power.

We beseech Thee to be with this people that they may be blessed by the work and service of this Minister, and may they give to him all due honor, encouragement, cooperation and support; through Jesus Christ our Lord. Amen.

HYMN: *(such as one of the following, the congregation standing)*
"O God Our Help in Ages Past"
"Saviour, More than Life"
"O Master, Let Me Walk with Thee"
"Jesus, I My Cross Have Taken"

SERMON:

OFFERING AND DEDICATION:

INDUCTED MINISTER'S REMARKS: *(Following the Dedication of the Offering, the newly inducted Minister shall be called upon for brief remarks at the Pulpit, after which he shall announce the closing Hymn.)*

HYMN: *(such as one of the following, the congregation standing through the Benediction)*
"Blest Be the Tie That Binds"
"Saviour, like a Shepherd Lead Us"
"On Our Way Rejoicing"
"Saviour, Again to Thy Dear Name"

THE BENEDICTION:
The peace of God, which passeth all understanding, keep your hearts and minds in the knowledge and love of God, and of His son Jesus Christ our Lord: And the blessing of God Almighty, the Father, the Son, and the Holy Spirit, be among you and remain with you always. Amen.

SERVICE FOR ORGANIZING A NEW CHURCH

HYMN
SCRIPTURE READING

Prayer
Acts of Organization
Offering and Dedication
Hymn
Benediction

When the establishment of a new Church is not undertaken by the appropriate official body of some denomination but by a group of interested Christians, the following procedure is recommended.

Those interested in organizing a Church should seek, preferably, the use of some convenient church building for this purpose. If this is not convenient, then the home of one of the interested persons may be used.

Selecting a Chairman and Clerk *pro tem* at some announced meeting prior to the organization of the Church, the interested persons should decide upon the following matters: What neighboring pastors and churches of the same Faith and Order shall be invited to counsel with them on the propriety and need of establishing a new Church in a given locality; the time and place of the meeting and the name of the Church to be organized.

The Clerk *pro tem* should then proceed to send out invitations to the Pastors of neighboring Churches decided upon, requesting that they bring at least two representatives of their Church with them, stating simply the purpose, time and place, and listing the names of the persons interested in organizing the Church. The neighboring pastors with the representatives shall form a Council.

On the day of the Council meeting, the following order may be used. The Chairman *pro tem* shall preside over the first three items.

Hymn:

Scripture Reading:

Prayer:

The Chairman pro tem shall briefly state the purpose of the meeting, and shall then turn it over to the Council.

ACTS OF ORGANIZATION

(1) *The* COUNCIL *shall organize itself, selecting a* MODERA-
TOR *to direct the further proceedings and a* CLERK *to record
them.*

(2) *The* COUNCIL *shall then call upon the* REPRESENTATIVE
*of the persons interested in organizing the Church to give the
group's reasons for so doing. The burden of the* REPRESENTA-
TIVE *shall be to establish and convince the* COUNCIL *of the need
for organizing a church in the locality in question, presenting
to them the persons with letters from other churches who will
become the charter members of the new Church. Their letters
shall be read by the* CLERK.

(3) *If the* COUNCIL *is convinced of the propriety and need,
they shall, by vote, approve this act.*

(4) *A Resolution shall now be prepared by the* COUNCIL
*and submitted to the persons interested for their approval and
signature. The Resolution should be formulated in the following
manner:*

Whereas we have called a Council, instituted of the following neighboring pastors and members [insert names here], rep-
resenting the following neighboring churches [insert names],
to counsel and to pray with us over the propriety and need of
organizing a new Church in this particular locality; and

Whereas, after due deliberation and prayer, the Council
has been convinced of the propriety and need of a new
Church in this locality and has approved the same; and

Whereas, we who are interested in the establishment of a
new Church in this particular locality have brought and
presented to this council our letters of dismission from
churches of the same Faith and Order:

Be it resolved that we do here and now enter upon the
organization of a new Church hereafter to be called [insert
name of church here] and adopt the following as our Covenant and Declaration of Faith [here shall be inserted the
Covenant and Declaration of Faith].

(5) After this Resolution, Covenant, and Declaration of

Faith are thoroughly discussed and finally approved, those constituting the new Church shall then sign the Resolution.

(6) The next step shall be to elect only the Officers who shall be necessary at this time to carry on the work of the new Church. These should include Deacons, Church Clerk, Superintendent of the Sunday school, Choir Director, Pianist or Organist, President of the Missionary Society and President of the Usher Board. If feasible, the Pastor shall also be chosen.

(7) Following this, the Right Hand of Fellowship shall be given to the members of the new Church. Then shall the door of the Church be opened to receive new members by Baptism or Christian Experience.

Offering and Dedication

Hymn

Benediction

SERVICE FOR DEDICATION OF A NEW CHURCH SITE

Opening Sentences

Invocation

Hymn

Scripture Readings from Old and New Testament

Brief Address

Presentation of Deed to Land

Consecration of the Land

   Responsive and Gloria Patri

   Prayer and Lord's Prayer

Benediction

Denominational and local Council of Churches representatives should be invited as participants whenever possible.

Let the people assemble at the appointed time at the place which has been purchased for a Church site, a platform from which all proceedings shall be conducted having been erected beforehand.

A large permanent sign marking the site and carrying the neces-
sary information about the proposed project should be made avail-
able for use during the Ceremony.

OPENING SENTENCES:

Our help is in the name of the Lord, who made heaven and
earth. — Psalm 124:8.

Truth shall spring out of the earth; and righteousness shall
look down from heaven. — Psalm 85:11.

The heavens are thine [O Lord], the earth also is thine: as for
the world and the fulness thereof, thou hast founded them.
Blessed be the Lord for evermore. Amen, and Amen. — Psalm
89:11, 52.

INVOCATION:

Almighty God, Creator and Father of us all, who hast put it in
our hearts and minds to prepare a way and to lift up a standard
for the people, grant unto us Thy approval of what we shall do
this day and in this place that all we have purposed and planned
may come to full and holy fruition; through Jesus Christ our
Lord. Amen.

HYMN: *(such as one of the following)*

"From All That Dwells below the Skies"
"All People That on Earth Do Dwell"

SCRIPTURE READING:

From the Old Testament

The earth is the Lord's, and the fulness thereof; the world,
and they that dwell therein.

For he hath founded it upon the seas, and established it upon
the floods.

Who shall ascend into the hill of the Lord? or who shall
stand in his holy place?

He that hath clean hands, and a pure heart; who hath not
lifted up his soul unto vanity, nor sworn deceitfully.

He shall receive the blessing from the Lord, and righteousness
from the God of his salvation.

This is the generation of them that seek him, that seek thy face, O Jacob. Selah.

Lift up your heads, O ye gates; and be ye lift up, ye everlasting doors; and the King of glory shall come in.

Who is this King of glory? The Lord strong and mighty, the Lord mighty in battle.

Lift up your heads, O ye gates; even lift them up, ye everlasting doors; and the King of glory shall come in.

Who is this King of glory? The Lord of hosts, he is the King of glory. Selah. — Psalm 24.

From the New Testament

Jesus Christ the same yesterday, and to day, and for ever.

By him therefore let us offer the sacrifice of praise to God continually, that is, the fruit of our lips giving thanks to his name.

But to do good and to communicate forget not: for with such sacrifices God is well pleased.

Now the God of peace, that brought again from the dead our Lord Jesus, that great shepherd of the sheep, through the blood of the everlasting covenant,

Make you perfect in every good work to do his will, working in you that which is wellpleasing in his sight, through Jesus Christ; to whom be glory for ever and ever. Amen. — Hebrews 13:8, 15-16, 20-21.

BRIEF ADDRESS: (*Here shall be set forth the purpose of the occasion, the plans and the hopes of the Congregation for itself and the community in which its new Church shall be situated.*)

PRESENTATION OF DEED TO THE LAND: (*A Representative of the Board of Trustees shall now present to the Minister the deed to the Land which has been purchased for the Church site. The Minister shall consecrate the Land in the following manner.*)

CONSECRATION OF THE LAND:

Responsive and Gloria Patri:

Minister:

This land shall be your possession before the Lord. — Numbers 32:22.

Defile not therefore the land which ye shall inhabit, where-in I dwell [saith the Lord]: for I the Lord dwell among the children of Israel. — Numbers 35:34.

People:

Surely the Lord is in this place.... this is none other but the house of God, and this is the gate of heaven.

Minister:

This stone, which I have set for a pillar (*directing large printed sign to be firmly set in the ground*), shall be God's house.
The Gloria Patri shall here be sung by the People.

Minister:

Let thy work [O Lord] appear unto thy servants,

People:

And thy glory unto their children.

Minister:

And let the beauty of the Lord our God be upon us:

People:

And establish thou the work of our hands upon us;

Unison:

Yea, the work of our hands establish thou it. — Psalm 90:16-17.

Prayer and Lord's Prayer:

Almighty and everlasting God, our heavenly Father, who didst create the heavens and the earth and all things therein; Thou who inhabitest eternity and whose Name is holy: We praise Thee. We give thanks to Thee. We adore Thee. We magnify Thee. For Thy goodness to us has been exceedingly great and Thy faithfulness has known no end. As Thou didst fulfill Thy word to former generations of those who have called upon Thee in faith and expectancy, hear now the prayer we make.

We thank Thee that this people assembled at this place have purposed in their hearts to erect here a House to Thee.

Be pleased, O God, to bless, direct and to prosper their efforts that they may find satisfaction in this holy work and joy in the sacrifices they shall make to achieve their ends. As they have met to dedicate this site to Thee, grant, O Lord God, that they themselves may be consecrated by the indwelling of the Holy Spirit so that they may undertake their holy task in full reliance upon Thy help, in a spirit of love and cooperation with each other, and with the blessing of community good will.

Most blessed and eternal God, our Father: As Thou in Thy providence hast blessed this people to acquire this land upon which to build Thee a House, be Thou pleased to accept now their dedication of it to this holy use and purpose. Since Thy presence alone can hallow any place, we beseech Thee to let Thy Spirit rest upon this ground. Consecrate it as a possession of Thy Church. Hallow it as a reservation in space to which this people may repair in future days, yea, in the years to come, for their accustomed meetings with Thee.

O eternal God, our blessed Redeemer and ever sure defense: Establish and defend the work of this Thy people. For without Thy aid no work of man can ever be firmly established; nor can its defense be sure.

Give to this people Thine assistance, O Holy One, and grant that the task they now envision for this place may one day soon become a reality; through Jesus Christ our Lord, who taught us when we pray to say:

Our Father which art in heaven, Hallowed be thy name. Thy kingdom come. Thy will be done in earth, as it is in heaven. Give us this day our daily bread. And forgive us our debts, as we forgive our debtors. And lead us not into temptation, but deliver us from evil: For thine is the kingdom, and the power, and the glory, for ever. Amen.

BENEDICTION

Grace be unto you, and peace, from God our Father, and from the Lord Jesus Christ. Amen. — I Corinthians 1:3.

SERVICE FOR BREAKING GROUND FOR
A NEW CHURCH

Opening Sentences
Invocation
Hymn
Readings from Old and New Testaments
Brief Address and Felicitations
Ground-Breaking Ceremony
    Responsive
    Prayer
    Breaking of Ground
Gloria Patri
Benediction

A platform, from which the Ground-Breaking Ceremony is to be conducted, should be erected beforehand on the site where the Church is to be built.

Denominational and local Council of Churches representatives should be invited to participate in this Ceremony whenever possible.

When the People have asesmbled at the hour appointed for the Ceremony, the Minister shall begin.

Opening Sentences:

Thus saith the Lord, The heaven is my throne, and the earth is my footstool: where is the house that ye build unto me? and where is the place of my rest? — Isaiah 66:1.

Shalt thou build me a house for me to dwell in? — II Samuel 7:5.

Now set your heart and your soul to seek the Lord your God; arise therefore, and build ye the sanctuary of the Lord God, to bring the ark of the covenant of the Lord, and the holy vessels of God, into the house that is to be built to the name of the Lord. — I Chronicles 22:19.

INVOCATION:

O gracious God, our Lord, without whose presence we meet together in vain: Bless us with the visitation of Thy Holy Spirit that the acts we shall perform here may be acceptable to Thee and an honor to Thy Holy Name; through Jesus Christ our Lord. Amen.

HYMN: *(such as one of the following)*
   "O Worship the King"
   "Praise to the Lord, the Almighty"
   "From All That Dwell below the Skies"

From the Old Testament

I

Furthermore David the king said unto all the congregation, Solomon my son, whom alone God hath chosen, is yet young and tender, and the work is great: for the palace is not for man, but for the Lord God.

Now I have prepared with all my might for the house of my God the gold for things to be made of gold, and the silver for things of silver, and the brass for things of brass, the iron for things of iron, and wood for things of wood; onyx stones, and stones to be set, glistering stones, and of divers colours, and all manner of precious stones, and marble stones in abundance.

Moreover, because I have set my affections to the house of my God, I have of mine own proper good, of gold and silver, which I have given to the house of my God, over and above all that I have prepared for the holy house,

Even three thousand talents of gold, of the gold of Ophir, and seven thousand talents of refined silver, to overlay the walls of the houses withal:

The gold for things of gold, and the silver for things of silver, and for all manner of work to be made by the hands of artificers. And who then is willing to consecrate his service this day unto the Lord?

Then the people rejoiced, for that they offered willingly, because with perfect heart they offered willingly to the Lord:

and David the king also rejoiced with great joy. — I Chronicles 29:1-5, 9.

II

I will extol thee, my God, O king; and I will bless thy name for ever and ever.

Every day will I bless thee; and I will praise thy name for ever and ever.

Great is the Lord, and greatly to be praised; and his greatness is unsearchable.

One generation shall praise thy works to another, and shall declare thy mighty acts.

I will speak of the glorious honour of thy majesty, and of thy wondrous works.

All thy works shall praise thee, O Lord; and thy saints shall bless thee.

They shall speak of the glory of thy kingdom, and talk of thy power;

To make known to the sons of men his mighty acts, and the glorious majesty of his kingdom.

Thy kingdom is an everlasting kingdom, and thy dominion endureth throughout all generations. — Psalm 145:1-5, 10-13.

III

(To be read responsively)

Minister:

Blessed be thou, Lord God of Israel our father, for ever and ever.

People:

Thine, O Lord, is the greatness, and the power, and the glory, and the victory, and the majesty; for all that is in the heaven and in the earth is thine; thine is the kingdom, O Lord, and thou art exalted as head above all.

Minister:

Both riches and honour come of thee, and thou reignest over all; and in thine hand is power and might; and in thine hand it is to make great, and to give strength unto all.

People:

Now therefore, our God, we thank thee, and praise thy glorious name.

Minister:

But who am I, and what is my people, that we should be able to offer so willingly after this sort? for all things come of thee, and of thine own have we given thee.

People:

For we are strangers before thee, and sojourners, as were all our fathers: our days on the earth are as a shadow, and there is none abiding.

Unison:

O Lord our God, all this store that we have prepared to build thee an house for thine holy name cometh of thine hand, and is all thine own.

— I Chronicles 29:10-16.

From the New Testament

I

Ye are the salt of the earth: but if the salt have lost his savour, wherewith shall it be salted? it is thenceforth good for nothing, but to be cast out, and to be trodden under foot of men.

Ye are the light of the world. A city that is set on an hill cannot be hid.

Neither do men light a candle, and put it under a bushel, but on a candlestick; and it giveth light unto all that are in the house.

Let your light so shine before men, that they may see your good works, and glorify your Father which is in heaven. — Matthew 5:13-16.

II

Another parable put he forth unto them, saying, The kingdom of heaven is like to a grain of mustard seed, which a man took, and sowed in his field:

Which indeed is the least of all seeds; but when it is grown, it is the greatest among herbs, and becometh a tree, so that the birds of the air come and lodge in the branches thereof.

Another parable spake he unto them; The kingdom of heaven is like unto leaven, which a woman took, and hid in three measures of meal, till the whole was leavened. — Matthew 13:31-33.

BRIEF ADDRESS: *(including the purpose of the occasion; why a Church is being built at this location; and what purpose and services the Congregation envision in their new church)*

Felicitations may follow here by church leaders and prominent citizens.

GROUND-BREAKING CEREMONY:

Responsive:

Minister:

Let us now prepare to build us an altar . . . that it may be a witness between us, and you, and our generations after us, that we might do the service of the Lord before him . . . ; that your children may not say to our children in time to come, Ye have no part in the Lord. — Joshua 22:26-27.

People:

Behold the pattern of the altar of the Lord, which our fathers made, not for burnt offerings, nor for sacrifices; but it is a witness between us and you. . . . It shall be a witness between us that the Lord is God. — Joshua 22:28,34.

Unison:

This day we perceive that the Lord is among us. — Joshua 22:31.

PRAYER:

O Lord God, Thou who through Thy Son has enjoined us to continue Thy work till Thou comest again: Preserve and prosper us Thy people to be faithful and to accomplish the task which, this day, we undertake in Thy Name. Let

Thy Holy Spirit accompany us that we may find in Him a sufficient guide, an unfailing strength, and a wisdom equal to the size of our task. Raise up friends for us, O God, and prosper those who support Thy work through our Church that we may always have a supply equal to our needs.

When the burden of our work grows increasingly heavy upon us and we are tempted to give up, be Thou pleased to lighten our burden by strengthening our spirit. When difficulties come and lack of understanding and conflict of desires hinder our efforts, work Thou, O heavenly Father, on our behalf and advance Thy cause in spite of us. When we cannot see our way clearly or know which way to take, be Thou, O God, our light and direct us in the right way. Stay with us, Lord God, to bless us, to uphold us, to inspire us, and to encourage us that the work of our hands may glorify Thee and be a blessing to many souls; through Jesus Christ our Lord. Amen.

BREAKING OF GROUND:
Now shall the person so designated break the ground upon which the Church edifice shall be erected. The People shall sing the Gloria Patri when this has been done.

THE BENEDICTION:
Now unto the King Eternal, immortal, invisible, the only wise God, be honour and glory forever and ever. Amen. — I Timothy 1:17.

SERVICE FOR LAYING THE CORNERSTONE OF A NEW CHURCH BUILDING

RESPONSIVE OF MINISTER AND PEOPLE

INVOCATION

HYMN

SCRIPTURE READING

BRIEF REMARKS

Act of Laying Cornerstone
   Responsive
   Depositing of Box
   Lowering and Sealing of Cornerstone
   Prayer
Hymn
Benediction

Preparation for laying the cornerstone should be made well in advance of the time appointed for the Ceremony. A platform should be erected from which all Proceedings may be directed. A metallic box, containing such things as the history of the Church, the names of the Building Committee, proceedings of a Business Meeting where the decision to build was recorded, and any other documents, papers or articles deemed desirable, should be available for depositing in the cavity left in the completed foundation for the Cornerstone. The cavity is at the right-hand corner or angle of the foundation to one facing the main entrance of the building.

The Cornerstone should have engraved on it the name of the Church, the year the stone is laid, the name of the Minister, and any other information considered desirable.

Denominational and local Council of Churches representatives, prominent citizens, the architect and builder, should be invited to participate in this Ceremony.

When the hour appointed for the Ceremony has arrived, the People being assembled, this or a similar Order shall be followed.

Responsive of Minister and People:

   The Minister:

      Thus said the Lord God, Behold, I lay in Zion for a foundation a stone, a tried stone, a precious cornerstone, a sure foundation. — Isaiah 28:16.

   The People:

      The stone which the builders refused is become the head stone of the corner. — Psalm 118:22.

The Minister:

This is the Lord's doing; it is marvellous in our eyes. — Psalm 118:23.

The People:

Glory be to the Father, and to the Son, and to the Holy Ghost: as it was in the beginning, is now and ever shall be, world without end. Amen.

INVOCATION:

O gracious heavenly Father, who withholdest nothing good from those who put their trust in Thee: open Thou our lips that our mouths may show forth Thy praise, for Thou hast made us glad through Thy work. Meet with us and rule in every heart that this day may be a day of grace and blessing to us; through Jesus Christ our Lord. Amen.

HYMN: *(such as one of the following)*

"The Church's One Foundation"
"Zion Stands with Hills Surrounded"
"Glorious Things of Thee Are Spoken"

SCRIPTURE READING:

For we are his workmanship, created in Christ Jesus unto good works, which God hath before ordained that we should walk in them.

Wherefore remember, that ye being in time past Gentiles in the flesh, who are called Uncircumcision by that which is called the Circumcision in the flesh made by hands;

That at that time ye were without Christ, being aliens from the commonwealth of Israel, and strangers from the covenants of promise, having no hope, and without God in the world:

But now in Christ Jesus ye who sometimes were far off are made nigh by the blood of Christ.

For he is our peace, who hath made both one, and hath broken down the middle wall of partition between us;

Having abolished in his flesh the enmity, even the law of commandments contained in ordinances; for to make in himself of twain one new man, so making peace;

And that he might reconcile both unto God in one body by the cross, having slain the enmity thereby:

And came and preached peace to you which were afar off, and to them that were nigh.

For through him we both have access by one Spirit unto the Father.

Now therefore ye are no more strangers and foreigners, but fellow citizens with the saints, and of the household of God;

And are built upon the foundation of the apostles and prophets, Jesus Christ himself being the chief corner stone;

In whom all the building fitly framed together groweth unto an holy temple in the Lord:

In whom ye also are builded together for an habitation of God through the Spirit. — Ephesians 2:10-22.

— or —

Wherefore laying aside all malice, and all guile, hypocrisies, and envies, and all evil speakings,

As newborn babes, desire the sincere milk of the word, that ye may grow thereby:

If so be ye have tasted that the Lord is gracious.

To whom coming, as unto a living stone, disallowed indeed of men, but chosen of God, and precious,

Ye also, as living stones, are built up a spiritual house, an holy priesthood, to offer up spiritual sacrifices, acceptable to God by Jesus Christ.

Wherefore also it is contained in the scripture, Behold, I lay in Zion a chief corner stone, elect, precious: and he that believeth on him shall not be confounded.

Unto you therefore which believe he is precious: but unto them which be disobedient, the stone which the builders disallowed, the same is made the head of the corner,

And a stone of stumbling, and a rock of offence, even to them which stumble at the word, being disobedient: whereunto also they were appointed.

But ye are a chosen generation, a royal priesthood, an holy nation, a peculiar people; that ye should show forth the praises of him who hath called you out of darkness into his marvellous light.

Which in time past were not a people, but are now the people of God: which had not obtained mercy, but now have obtained mercy. — I Peter 2:1-10.

BRIEF REMARKS: *(regarding the purpose of the occasion and welcoming the special guests)*

ACT OF LAYING THE CORNERSTONE:
Responsive:

The Minister:
But thou, O Lord, shalt endure for ever; and thy remembrance unto all generations. — Psalm 102:12.

The People:
Thou shalt arise, and have mercy upon Zion: for the time to favour her, yea, the set time, is come. — v. 13.

The Minister:
For thy servants take pleasure in her stones, and favour the dust thereof. — v. 14.

The People:
So the heathen shall fear the name of the Lord, and all the kings of the earth thy glory. — v. 15.

The Minister:
When the Lord shall build up Zion, he shall appear in his glory. — v. 16.

The People:
He will regard the prayer of the destitute, and not despise their prayer. — v. 17.

Unison:
This shall be written for the generation to come: and the people which shall be created shall praise the Lord. — v. 18.

Depositing of Box:
At this point the person designated to do so shall read in the hearing of all the People the contents sealed in the metallic

box and then place it in the cavity of the foundation. These
or similar words he shall say.

Designate:

Let these documents and mementos be preserved as a witness
to our children's children of our triumph in the work of God's
hand. Amen.

Lowering and Sealing:

Then shall those persons designated to lower the cornerstone
into place and to seal it with cement and trowel be so directed
by the Minister or Officiant. Here shall follow a Prayer in
these or similar words.

PRAYER:

Almighty and eternal God, who didst lay the foundations of
the earth and the cornerstone thereof: Establish Thou the
work of our hands; for except Thou buildest this House for
us, we who labor build in vain. Bless the foundation the
builders have built as our hearts are lifted in praise to Thee
for the protection Thou hast given the workers and the willing and generous spirit with which this people have offered
their substance that a House may be erected to Thy Holy
Name. Prosper them, O Lord most High, that this work may
be continued and fully completed. Save the workmen from
grievous accidents and their unfinished work from disaster.
And may all the hopes of Thy people on Thee be founded;
through Jesus Christ our Lord, the Rock of Ages and our
Masterbuilder who buildeth even unto now. Amen.

HYMN: *(such as one of the following)*

"Rock of Ages"
"My Hope Is Built on Nothing Less"
"How Firm a Foundation"
"Lift Him Up"

BENEDICTION:

The grace of the Lord Jesus Christ, the love of God, and the
communion of the Holy Spirit, be with you all. Amen.

SERVICE FOR THE DEDICATION OF A NEW CHURCH BUILDING

CALL TO WORSHIP

INVOCATION

HYMN

OLD TESTAMENT LESSON

HYMN OR ANTHEM

NEW TESTAMENT LESSON

PRESENTATION OF KEYS TO THE MINISTER

PRAYER OF DEDICATION

HYMN

SERMON

HYMN

OFFERING AND DEDICATION

DOXOLOGY

BENEDICTION

It is desirable that the various parts of this Dedication be assigned to Ministers who are members of the Church to be dedicated as well as to Ministers of other Churches.

When the hour arrives for the Service to begin, the Minister shall call the Congregation to worship and offer an Invocation. The Congregation shall stand through the singing of the first Hymn.

CALL TO WORSHIP:

Behold, the tabernacle of God is with men, and he will dwell with them, and they shall be his people, and God himself shall be with them, and be their God. — Revelation 21:3.

— *or* —

One thing have [we] desired of the Lord, that will [we] seek after; that [we] may dwell in the house of the Lord all the days of [our] life, to behold the beauty of the Lord, and to inquire in his temple. — Psalm 27:4.

INVOCATION:

Almighty and everlasting God, as we are now met together for the first time in Thy House which has been built for divine worship and Thy glory, we beseech Thee to pour out Thy Spirit upon us that we may be found in Thy presence with a grateful heart and a contrite and humble spirit. Help us worthily to magnify Thy Name and to rejoice in Thy faithfulness; through Jesus Christ our Lord. Amen.

HYMN: *(such as one of the following)*

"Praise the Lord, His Glories Show"
"Rejoice the Lord Is King"
"Praise to the Living God"
"All Hail the Power of Jesus' Name"
"Praise to the Lord, the Almighty"
"O for a Heart to Praise My God"

OLD TESTAMENT LESSON:

And Solomon stood before the altar of the Lord in the presence of all the congregation of Israel, and spread forth his hands toward heaven:

And he said, Lord God of Israel, there is no God like thee, in heaven above, or on earth beneath, who keepest covenant and mercy with thy servants that walk before thee with all their heart:

Who hast kept with thy servant David my father that thou promisedst him: thou spakest also with thy mouth, and hast fulfilled it with thine hand, as it is this day.

Therefore, now, Lord God of Israel, keep with thy servant David my father that thou promisedst him, saying, There shall not fail thee a man in my sight to sit on the throne of Israel; so that thy children take heed to their way, that they walk before me as thou hast walked before me.

And now, O God of Israel, let thy word, I pray thee, be verified, which thou spakest unto thy servant David my father. But will God indeed dwell on the earth? behold, the heaven

and heaven of heavens cannot contain thee; how much less this
house that I have builded?

Yet have thou respect unto the prayer of thy servant, and to
his supplication, O Lord my God, to hearken unto the cry and to
the prayer, which thy servant prayeth before thee to day:

That thine eyes may be open toward this house night and
day, even toward the place of which thou hast said, My name
shall be there: that thou mayest hearken unto the prayer which
thy servant shall make toward this place.

And hearken thou to the supplication of thy servant, and of
thy people Israel, when they shall pray toward this place: and
hear thou in heaven thy dwelling place: and when thou hearest, forgive. — I Kings 8:22-30.

— or —

How amiable are thy tabernacles, O Lord of hosts!

My soul longeth, yea, even fainteth for the courts of the Lord:
my heart and my flesh crieth out for the living God.

Yea, the sparrow hath found a house, and the swallow a
nest for herself, where she may lay her young, even thine altars,
O Lord of hosts, my King, and my God.

Blessed are they that dwell in thy house: they will be still
praising thee. Selah.

Blessed is the man whose strength is in thee; in whose heart
are the ways of them.

Who passing through the valley of Baca make it a well; the
rain also filleth the pools.

They go from strength to strength, every one of them in Zion
appeareth before God.

O Lord God of hosts, hear my prayer: give ear, O God of
Jacob. Selah.

Behold, O God our shield, and look upon the face of thine
anointed.

For a day in thy courts is better than a thousand. I had rather
be a doorkeeper in the house of my God, than to dwell in the
tents of wickedness.

For the Lord God is a sun and shield: the Lord will give

grace and glory: no good thing will he withhold from them that walk uprightly.

O Lord of hosts, blessed is the man that trusteth in thee. — Psalm 84.

Hymn or Anthem: *(about the Church)*

New Testament Lesson:

When Jesus came into the coasts of Caesarea Philippi, he asked his disciples, saying, Whom do men say that I the Son of man am?

And they said, Some say that thou art John the Baptist; some, Elias; and others, Jeremias, or one of the prophets.

He saith unto them, But whom say ye that I am?

And Simon Peter answered and said, Thou art the Christ, the Son of the living God.

And Jesus answered and said unto him, Blessed art thou, Simon Bar-jona: for flesh and blood hath not revealed it unto thee, but my Father which is in heaven.

And I say also unto thee, That thou art Peter, and upon this rock I will build my church; and the gates of hell shall not prevail against it.

And I will give unto thee the keys of the kingdom of heaven: and whatsoever thou shalt bind on earth shall be bound in heaven: and whatsoever thou shalt loose on earth shall be loosed in heaven.

Then charged he his disciples that they should tell no man that he was Jesus the Christ. — Matthew 16:13-20.

— *or* —

For we are labourers together with God: ye are God's husbandry, ye are God's building.

According to the grace of God which is given unto me, as a wise masterbuilder, I have laid the foundation, and another buildeth thereon. But let every man take heed how he buildeth thereupon.

For other foundation can no man lay than that is laid, which is Jesus Christ.

Now if any man build upon this foundation gold, silver, precious stones, wood, hay, stubble.

Every man's work shall be made manifest: for the day shall declare it, because it shall be revealed by fire; and the fire shall try every man's work of what sort it is.

If any man's work abide which he hath built thereupon, he shall receive a reward.

If any man's work shall be burned, he shall suffer loss: but he himself shall be saved; yet so as by fire.

Know ye not that ye are the temple of God, and that the Spirit of God dwelleth in you?

If any man defile the temple of God, him shall God destroy; for the temple of God is holy, which temple ye are.

Let no man deceive himself. If any man among you seemeth to be wise in this world, let him become a fool, that he may be wise.

For the wisdom of this world is foolishness with God. For it is written, He taketh the wise in their own craftiness.

And again, The Lord knoweth the thoughts of the wise, that they are vain.

Therefore let no man glory in men. For all things are yours;

Whether Paul, or Apollos, or Cephas, or the world, or life, or death, or things present, or things to come; all are yours;

And ye are Christ's; and Christ is God's. — I Corinthians 3:9-23.

PRESENTATION OF KEYS OF THE CHURCH: *(by a Representative of the Building Committee)*

Building Representative:

I present to you, on behalf of the Building Committee, the keys of this House, erected for divine worship and the glory of God. May it provide you and this Congregation with the necessary conveniences and facilities for making most effective the ministry of the Word and the many services that shall be carried on here.

The Minister:

On behalf of this Congregation and with sincere commendation to you and your Committee for the Christian and efficient manner in which you have accomplished this task — with, of course, the strong backing of many members of this Church — I accept these keys in token of the high mission entrusted to us. Now let us dedicate this House to the Worship of God.

PRAYER OF DEDICATION:

Almighty and everlasting God, our heavenly Father who, in Thy Son, art the Rock upon which Thy Church is built: We thank Thee for this House which has been built for Thy honor and service. Thy goodness hath attended the work and the workmen [and no accidents have occurred to sadden our spirits]. We praise Thee. We glorify Thee. We magnify Thy Holy Name. We now solemnly and gratefully dedicate this House to Thee, O Lord God, and we pray that Thou wilt consecrate it and make it holy by Thy indwelling. Grant that it will be in truth and deed a House dedicated to Thy service and glory.

We pray for those who will minister before Thee and Thy people in this House. May they be inspired by the things that are holy to lead a devout and godly life. Endow them with wisdom and knowledge, courage and power, patience and humility, in the discharge of all their duties.

We pray for all those who worship here now and for those Thy children who, in the years to come, shall worship in this Zion. Grant that here the Gospel may always be preached with power, Thy Ordinances observed with reverence and Thy Spirit obeyed as the uniting power of Christian hearts. Inspire all those who may worship here to a praise worthy of Thee. Grant that their confessions and supplications may be according to Thy will and that they may find here the blessing of Thy pardoning grace, Thy comforting Word, their rest and a peace which passeth all understanding.

Let this House, we beseech Thee, be a place of hallowed memories, a place of fellowship with Thee and the saints on earth and in heaven, and the birthplace of many souls. Arise, O Lord, into Thy rest, Thou and the ark of Thy strength; we pray for Jesus' sake, who taught us when we pray to say:

Our Father which art in heaven, Hallowed be thy name. Thy

kingdom come. Thy will be done in earth, as it is in heaven. Give us this day our daily bread. And forgive us our debts, as we forgive our debtors. And lead us not into temptation, but deliver us from evil: For thine is the kingdom, and the power, and the glory, forever. Amen.

HYMN: (a Hymn about the Church, such as one of the following, the congregation standing)

   "The Church's One Foundation"
   "I Love Thy Kingdom, Lord"
   "Glorious Things of Thee Are Spoken"
   "O Where Are Kings and Empires Now"

SERMON:

HYMN: (of praise)

OFFERING AND DEDICATION:

DOXOLOGY: (the congregation standing for this and the Benediction)

BENEDICTION:

Now unto him that is able to do exceeding abundantly above all that we ask or think, according to the power that worketh in us, unto him be glory in the church by Christ Jesus throughout all ages, world without end. Amen.

SERVICE FOR BURNING THE MORTGAGE ON A CHURCH BUILDING

CALL TO WORSHIP

INVOCATION

HYMN

OLD TESTAMENT LESSON

GLORIA PATRI

NEW TESTAMENT LESSON

PRAYER

ANTHEM

SERMON OR ADDRESS
MORTGAGE-BURNING CEREMONY
  HYMN
  ACT OF PRAISE
  ACT OF THANKSGIVING
  DOXOLOGY
  OFFERING
BENEDICTION

*When the hour arrives for the Service to begin, the Minister
shall give the Call to Worship and offer the Invocation. The Congregation shall stand through the singing of the first hymn.*

CALL TO WORSHIP:
  Let us worship God.
  The Lord hath done great things for us; whereof we are glad.
  — Psalm 126:3.

                    — *or* —

  O give thanks unto the Lord; call upon his name: make known
  his deeds among the people. Sing unto him, sing psalms unto
  him: talk ye of all his wondrous works. — Psalm 105:1-2.

INVOCATION:
  Almighty and gracious God: As we are now met to present to
  Thee a more suitable offering — this unencumbered building for
  divine worship — we would pray that Thou grant us the guidance of Thy Holy Spirit that the offering we present to Thee
  this day in word and act may be acceptable in Thy sight;
  through Jesus Christ our Lord. Amen.

HYMN: *(of praise, such as one of the following)*
    "Praise to the Lord, the Almighty"
    "Praise to the Living God"
    "Come We That Love the Lord"
    "O Bless the Lord, My Soul"
    "Open Now Thy Gates of Beauty"

OLD TESTAMENT LESSON:

Wherefore David blessed the Lord before all the congregation: and David said, Blessed be thou, Lord God of Israel our father, for ever and ever.

Thine, O Lord, is the greatness, and the power, and the glory, and the victory, and the majesty: for all that is in the heaven and in the earth is thine; thine is the kingdom, O Lord, and thou art exalted as head above all.

Both riches and honour come of thee, and thou reignest over all; and in thine hand is power and might; and in thine hand it is to make great, and to give strength unto all.

Now therefore, our God, we thank thee, and praise thy glorious name.

But who am I, and what is my people, that we should be able to offer so willingly after this sort? for all things come of thee, and of thine own have we given thee.

For we are strangers before thee, and sojourners, as were all our fathers: our days on the earth are as a shadow, and there is none abiding. — I Chronicles 29:10-15.

GLORIA PATRI:

NEW TESTAMENT LESSON:

I beseech you therefore, brethren, by the mercies of God that ye present your bodies a living sacrifice, holy, acceptable unto God, which is your reasonable service.

And be not conformed to this world: but be ye transformed by the renewing of your mind, that ye may prove what is that good, and acceptable, and perfect, will of God.

For I say, through the grace given unto me, to every man that is among you, not to think of himself more highly than he ought to think; but to think soberly, according as God hath dealt to every man the measure of faith.

For as we have many members in one body, and all members have not the same office:

So we, being many, are one body in Christ, and every one members one of another.

Having then gifts differing according to the grace that is

given to us, whether prophecy, let us prophesy according to the proportion of faith;

Or ministry, let us wait on our ministering: or he that teacheth, on teaching;

Or he that exhorteth, on exhortation: he that giveth, let him do it with simplicity; he that ruleth, with diligence; he that sheweth mercy, with cheerfulness.

Let love be without dissimulation. Abhor that which is evil; cleave to that which is good.

Be kindly affectioned one to another with brotherly love; in honour preferring one another;

Not slothful in business; fervent in spirit; serving the Lord;

Rejoicing in hope; patient in tribulation; continuing instant in prayer;

Distributing to the necessity of saints; given to hospitality.

Bless them which persecute you: bless, and curse not.

Rejoice with them that do rejoice, and weep with them that weep.

Be of the same mind one toward another. Mind not high things, but condescend to men of low estate. Be not wise in your own conceits.

Recompense to no man evil for evil. Provide things honest in the sight of all men. — Romans 12:1-17.

PRAYER: (by a representative of a sister church)

O God, our heavenly Father, who didst direct Thy people of old to make Thee a house to dwell in and who hast always been pleased to hallow the place Thy people have offered for the glory of Thy name: We meet on this occasion in joy and with thankful hearts that we are now blessed to offer Thee an unencumbered house for the perpetual praise of Thy holy name. It is Thou, O Lord God, who hast made possible this accomplishment. For Thou didst put it into the hearts of this people to pay for this place and hast provided them with the means so to do. When weary of the load, impatient with results, and discouraged by obstructions and lack of support, the faithful of this congregation have been upheld and sustained by Thy presence and goodness. Thou hast not allowed any adverse power to overwhelm them, and thus hast brought them to this day successful in their efforts and triumphant in spirit.

Bless, we would beseech Thee, all those who have had a mind to work and to continue in the struggle to the completion of this task. Bless them with joy in believing in Thy providence and with a fruitful, continually vital fellowship as a congregation that there may always be glory in Thy church and honor always freely given to Thy name; through Jesus Christ our Lord. Amen.

ANTHEM: *(by the Choir, such as one of the following)*

"Let Mount Zion Rejoice," J. Herbert
"Alleluia," Charles D. Coleman
"Praise Ye the Lord," Randegger
"Gloria," from the *Twelfth Mass,* Mozart
"Thanks Be to God" (arranged for Chorus), Handel
"Hallelujah," from the *Mount of Olives,* Beethoven
"Thanks Be to God," from the *Elijah,* Mendelssohn

SERMON OR TALK:

THE MORTGAGE-BURNING CEREMONY:

Hymn:

The Minister shall have brought to him to be placed on the altar the mortgage document in a fireproof receptacle. As this is being done, the Congregation may sing a hymn such as one of the following:

"God of Our Fathers, Whose Almighty Hand"
"The Bounties, Gracious Lord"
"We Give Thee but Thine Own"
"I Love Thy Kingdom, Lord"
"God of Our Life, through All the Circling Years"

Act of Praise:

Following appropriate words of praise to God and commendation of a faithful membership, the Minister, directing the Congregation to stand, may lead them in an Act of Praise.

Minister:

Praise ye the Lord. Praise God in His sanctuary: praise him in the firmament of his power.

People:

Praise him for his mighty acts: praise him according to his excellent greatness.

Minister:

Let everything that hath breath praise the Lord.

People:

Praise ye the Lord.

Act of Thanksgiving:

Minister:

Let us now thank God for our accomplishment through His help which has made this occasion possible. (*Let there be a brief pause after each bidding for the Congregation's silent response.*)

Let us thank God for church officers and committee members who have given dedicated, conscientious and effective leadership in both the temporal and spiritual affairs of our church during the liquidation of our debts. (*Pause*)

Let us thank God for faithful and loyal members, young and old, who with patience and sacrifice have made this offering of a debt-free house of worship to God possible. (*Pause*)

Let us thank God for the prayers and financial support of friends and for many community contacts which encouraged us and advanced our efforts. (*Pause*)

Receive, O God, the meditations of our hearts and our sacrifices of thanksgiving as our sincere and willing offering to Thee; through Jesus Christ our Lord. Amen.

Minister:

Now hear what the Lord God doth say: I have heard thy prayer and thy supplication, that thou hast made before me. I have hallowed this house, which thou hast built, to put my name there for ever; and mine eyes and mine heart shall be there perpetually. — I Kings 9:3.

Because we cannot offer to God what is not ours, we have completely liquidated the indebtedness on this house which we have built for God. To Him we now offer it, unencumbered and wholly ours. We burn this mortgage in symbolic expression of our gift cleansed and wholly presented to God.

(At this point, the person so designated will set fire to the mortgage document to be burned in the recepticle containing it. There shall be silence until the document is completely consumed and the fire is gone out.)

Doxology: *(the Congregation led by the Choir)*

Offering:

Following the Doxology, the Congregation shall bring an offering to the altar to complete the offering they make to God and to conclude the mortgage-burning ceremony.

When all the offerings have been received, the Congregation shall sing, "All things come of Thee, O Lord, and of Thine own have we given Thee. Amen."

BENEDICTION:

The grace of the Lord Jesus Christ, and the love of God, and the communion of the Holy Spirit, be with you all. Amen.

SECTION SIX

Ministering to the Sick and Shut-In

GUIDING PRINCIPLES AND PRACTICAL SUGGESTIONS

Whether in the home, the hospital, or some other institution, the Minister should not neglect to visit the sick and the shut-in. It is in this area of service that the Minister will find not only some of his greatest challenges and deepest rewards but also some of his greatest opportunities for personal spiritual growth, his development of effectual preaching power, and the highest conception of what constitutes a sermon.

The sick and the shut-in are usually most highly receptive to spiritual truths and the ministries represented by the man of God. The Minister, therefore, should give as much time as is practicable to his visitation ministry, equipped in his mind and heart with appropriate Scriptures and prayers to meet all conditions of the sick and shut-in. The more appropriate Scriptures and prayers he can have in his head and heart, the more effective he is likely to be.

When visiting the hospital or home, the Minister should be careful to see that his visit or what he does upon his visit does not in any way interfere with what the patient's physician has prescribed or desires for him. The comfort and recovery of the sick patient, not the minister's status, is of foremost importance. Therefore, in these matters, the Minister must defer to the physician and seek his guidance in ministering to the sick patient.

The Minister's visit of the sick should be brief, not more than a few minutes. With the convalescing and the shut-in, his visit may be a little more extended. His briefest stay should be with the very sick, and the situation should determine whether he recites a brief Scripture and utters a brief prayer or not. Not all sick visits should end in audible prayer and the reading of Scripture verses. The Minister's presence, and a touch of his hand, will sometimes be all that is required to aid the sick patient spiritually. The visits of the Minister to the sick and shut-in will really be quite self-regulatory. Many other pressing duties, added to the time consumed in getting from home to home or hospital to hospital, will not leave him with an abundance of time he can lavishly share even among those who truly need his ministry.

When the Minister visits, he should not give the impression that he is in a hurry, even though this may be the case. Let him rest his hat and his coat, when the weather requires him to have them. Let him sit down or stand at a position which will make it convenient for the patient to see him and chat with him, if he so desires. The conversation, the reading of Scriptures, and the uttering of prayer, all should be done in an unhurried manner, although only a few minutes may actually be consumed in the whole visit.

In the ministry to the convalescing and shut-in, recorded excerpts from the service of worship or specially recorded meditations, none of which should exceed fifteen minutes, are particularly effective. In all cases a copy of some simply prepared and printed daily devotional material, left for their use when they feel well enough to read it, will prove an effective spiritual aid.

MEDITATIONS AND PRAYERS
For General Use

— 1 —

Preserve me, O God: for in thee do I put my trust.

The Lord is the portion of mine inheritance and of my cup: thou maintainest my lot.

I have set the Lord always before me: because he is at my right hand, I shall not be moved.

Therefore my heart is glad, and my glory rejoiceth: my flesh also shall rest in hope.

Thou wilt show me the path of life: in thy presence is fulness of joy; at thy right hand there are pleasures for evermore. — Psalm 16:1, 5, 8-9, 11.

Let us pray:

Most merciful and strong God, our heavenly Father, who art

Lord over all Thy works: Preserve us Thy children who art fashioned by Thy hand and called by Thy name. Let Thy glory appear unto Thy servants, even the light and the help of Thy countenance; for without Thy favor, we despair. Without Thy help, we faint and fall. Grant that we may submit our will to Thine and commit ourselves to Thy keeping. And after we have suffered a while, be Thou pleased to perfect, stablish, strengthen, and settle us; through Jesus Christ our Lord. Amen.

— 2 —

It is of the Lord's mercies that we are not consumed, because his compassions fail not.

They are new every morning: great is thy faithfulness.

The Lord is my portion, saith my soul; therefore will I hope in him.

The Lord is good unto them that wait for him, to the soul that seeketh him.

It is good that a man should both hope and quietly wait for the salvation of the Lord. — Lamentations 3:22-26.

Let us pray:

Almighty God, our heavenly Father, who art rich in mercy: Be pleased to overrule the ills of life for our good. Let Thy mercy support us in our infirmities and Thy spirit guide us in our darkness. Make us strong in our trust of Thee and confident in our sure deliverance. Be Thou our portion and during our season of waiting, O gracious God, assure us that Thou wilt keep us in the secret place of Thy mercy; through Jesus Christ our Lord. Amen.

— 3 —

The Lord is my light and my salvation; whom shall I fear? the Lord is the strength of my life; of whom shall I be afraid?

For in the time of trouble he shall hide me in his pavilion: in the secret of his tabernacle shall he hide me; he shall set me up upon a rock.

Hear, O Lord, when I cry with my voice: have mercy also upon me, and answer me.— Psalm 27:1, 5, 7.

Let us pray:

Almighty God, our heavenly Father, who art the Father of
lights: Mercifully grant to us, through the gift of Thy Holy Spirit,
light to enlighten our mind and to illumine our heart that we may
be saved from error and doubt. Let Thy light rise up in our darkness so that the ills that beset us may not overwhelm us. Lay Thine
hand upon us that we may know that Thou art with us. Yea, guide
us through the snares of our adversities that we may not dishonor
Thee. And in the midst of the fire of our affliction, walk with us
that we may not be consumed; we pray through Jesus Christ our
Lord. Amen.

— 4 —

Who shall separate us from the love of Christ? shall tribulation,
or distress, or persecution, or famine, or nakedness, or peril, or
sword?

Nay, in all these things we are more than conquerors through
him that loved us.

For I am persuaded, that neither death, nor life, nor angels, nor
principalities, nor powers, nor things present, nor things to come,

Nor height, nor depth, nor any other creature, shall be able to
separate us from the love of God, which is in Christ Jesus our
Lord. Amen. — Romans 8:35, 37-39.

Let us pray:

Almighty and everlasting God, our heavenly Father, who hast
shown us, through the gift of Thine only begotten Son, the depth
and greatness of Thy love for us: Thou hast also shown us, in
His suffering and death, what rough paths the feet of love and
obedience may trod. Teach us the meaning of suffering, love and
obedience that we may overcome any foe which seeks to separate
us from Thy love. Grant us such fellowship with Christ, Thy
Son, in His sufferings that we may gladly and triumphantly bear
our own; we pray in the Name of Jesus Christ our Lord. Amen.

— 5 —

Let not your heart be troubled: ye believe in God, believe also
in me.

And I will pray the Father, and he shall give you another Comforter, that he may abide with you for ever;

Even the Spirit of truth; whom the world cannot receive, because it seeth him not, neither knoweth him: but ye know him; for he dwelleth with you, and shall be in you.

I will not leave you comfortless: I will come to you. — John 14:1, 16-18.

Let us pray:

O merciful and strong God, our Father, who inclineth Thine ear to all who call upon Thy Name: We thank Thee that Thou hast promised that we should not be left comfortless, but that Thou wouldst come to us. In Thy promises, O merciful Father, we hope and earnestly look with expectation toward this fulfillment. Speak to us, and we shall hear Thee. Teach us, and we shall willingly learn of Thee; mould us, and we shall completely submit to Thee; and heal us, O gracious God, and we shall be a living testimony to Thee; through Jesus Christ our Lord. Amen.

For Those in Physical or Mental Anguish

— 1 —

Trust in the Lord with all thine heart; and lean not unto thine own understanding.

In all thy ways acknowledge him, and he shall direct thy paths.

Commit thy way unto the Lord; trust also in him; and he shall bring it to pass.

And he shall bring forth thy righteousness as the light, and thy judgment as the noonday.

Rest in the Lord, and wait patiently for him. . . .

The Lord knoweth the days of the upright: and their inheritance shall be for ever.

They shall not be ashamed in the evil time: and in the days of famine they shall be satisfied. — Proverbs 3:5-6; Psalm 37:5-7, 18-19.

Let us pray:

O God, who didst give us Thy Spirit to strengthen us inwardly when the struggle is fierce within: Grant us faith to subdue our anguish of body and mind. Grant us the aid we need to leave the condition of our body and the turmoil of our spirit in Thy care. Help us to give ourselves over to Thy keeping; through Jesus Christ our Lord. Amen.

— 2 —

Behold the fowls of the air: for they sow not, neither do they reap, nor gather into barns; yet your heavenly Father feedeth them. Are ye not much better than they?

Which of you by taking thought can add one cubit unto his stature?

Take therefore no thought for the morrow: for the morrow shall take thought for the things of itself. Sufficient unto the day is the evil thereof.

Casting all your care upon him [the Lord], for he careth for you. — Matthew 6:26-27, 34; I Peter 5:7.

Let us pray:

O God, our soul is distressed with anxiety. We are too much concerned with the things that should be left with Thee. Help us to free ourselves from anxiety over the things which are not in our power to change or control. Teach us, O heavenly Father, how to cast all our care upon Thee and to trust Thy providence; we pray through our Lord Jesus Christ. Amen.

— 3 —

Why art thou cast down, O my soul? and why art thou disquieted in me? hope thou in God: for I shall yet praise him for the help of his countenance.

O my God, my soul is cast down within me. . . .

Yet the Lord will command his lovingkindness in the daytime, and in the night his song shall be with me, and my prayer unto the God of my life.

Why art thou cast down, O my soul? and why art thou disquieted within me? hope thou in God: for I shall yet praise him, who is the health of my countenance, and my God. — Psalm 42:5-6, 8, 11.

Let us pray:

O God, our spirit is beset with discouragement. Our illness has been long and worrisome. It has been difficult to take our mind off ourselves and to save ourselves from self-pity. But Thou, O Lord God, canst help us in our distresses and save us from discouragement. Be Thou pleased to help us so that we may rest underneath the protective care of Thy lovingkindness; through Jesus Christ our Lord, we pray. Amen.

— 4 —

What time I am afraid, I will trust in thee.

In God I will praise his word, in God I have put my trust; I will not fear what flesh can do unto me.

My soul, wait thou only upon God; for my expectation is from him.

He only is my rock and my salvation: he is my defense; I shall not be moved.

In God is my salvation and my glory: the rock of my strength, and my refuge, is in God. — Psalm 56:3-4; 62:5-7.

Let us pray:

O God, our Father, our heart and mind are full of fear. We have struggled to rise above the things that make us afraid, but our spirit is not relieved. We end each struggle still afraid. We know that, through faith in the power of Thy Spirit, we may overcome fear, but our faith has not been strong enough. We come as little children before Thee, O God, pleading to be taught how not to be afraid when we are so afflicted. Help us, Lord God, and give us a faith that walks without fear, even in our darkest hour; we beseech Thee through Jesus Christ our Lord. Amen.

— 5 —

Thou wilt keep him in perfect peace, whose mind is stayed on thee: because he trusteth in thee.

Trust ye in the Lord for ever: for in the Lord Jehovah is everlasting strength.

For thus saith the Lord God, the Holy One of Israel; in returning and rest shall ye be saved; in quietness and in confidence shall be your strength: and ye would not.

Fear not: for I am with thee. . . . — Isaiah 26:3-4; 30:15; 43:5.

Let us pray:

O merciful God, we need a stronger faith and a deepened trust in Thee, for our spirit is restless with worry and anxiety. We need the quiet and the calm of Thy refreshing Spirit. Breathe Thou upon us, O Breath of God. Breathe peace into our soul. When our spirit is cast down and disquieted within us, have compassion upon us, and comfort us with the remembrance of Thy precious promises; through our Lord Jesus Christ. Amen.

— 6 —

Rejoice in the Lord alway: and again I say, Rejoice.

Be careful for nothing; but in every thing by prayer and supplication with thanksgiving let your requests be made known unto God.

And the peace of God, which passeth all understanding, shall keep your hearts and minds through Christ Jesus.

But my God shall supply all your need according to his riches in glory by Christ Jesus.

Now unto God and our Father be glory for ever and ever. Amen. — Philippians 4:4, 6-7, 19-20.

Let us pray:

O God, help us in all things and at all times to rejoice in Thee. Let our prayer be one of thanksgiving always for all that Thou sendest us of joy or sorrow, of health or pain. Teach us to submit to Thy will in all things, and to be content in all changes of our life. Teach us to read our duty in Thy providence and to know what is in our heart through trial. Grant that, in affliction, we may be confident, patient and hopeful, trusting in Thee; through our Lord Jesus Christ. Amen.

For Those Seeking Forgiveness

— 1 —

For God so loved the world, that he gave his only begotten Son, that whosoever believeth in him should not perish, but have ever-lasting life.

For God sent not his Son into the world to condemn the world; but that the world through him might be saved.

He that believeth on him is not condemned: but he that believeth not is condemned already, because he hath not believed in the name of the only begotten Son of God.

But if we walk in the light, as he is in the light, we have fellowship one with another, and the blood of Jesus Christ his Son cleanseth us from all sin.

If we confess our sins, he is faithful and just to forgive us our sins, and to cleanse us from all unrighteousness. — John 3:16-18; John 1:7, 9.

Let us pray:

O Lord God, merciful and gracious, long-suffering and plenteous in mercy, who hast made known the exceeding riches of Thy grace to us through Thy Son: Remember not our former iniquities as we plead for Thy forgiveness and the healing of our body. We know that Thou art ready to forgive whosoever will, in sincerity and truth, repent of his sins. We confess our sins before Thee, O God, and pray for Thy pardoning grace that our soul may be restored in favor with Thee and our body blessed with Thy saving health; we pray in the Name of Jesus Christ our Lord. Amen.

— 2 —

Seek ye the Lord while he may be found, call ye upon him while he is near:

Let the wicked forsake his way, and the unrighteous man his thoughts: and let him return unto the Lord, and he will have mercy upon him; and to our God, for he will abundantly pardon.

Surely he hath borne our griefs, and carried our sorrows: yet we did esteem him stricken, smitten of God, and afflicted.

But he was wounded for our trangressions, he was bruised for our iniquities: the chastisement of our peace was upon him; and with his stripes we are healed. — Isaiah 55:6-7; 53:4-5.

Let us pray:

O great and merciful God, our Father, who art a God, ready to pardon, slow to anger and of great kindness: We confess that we have not desired or cared for Thee nor sought for Thee in times past. But we come to Thee now with a broken heart and a contrite spirit. Thy Word hath told us, O God, that such a heart and spirit, Thou wouldst not despise. Hide not Thy face from us, O heavenly Father, but out of the greatness of Thy love and mercy, own and accept us as Thy child; through Jesus Christ our Lord, we pray. Amen.

— 3 —

Have mercy upon me, O God, according to thy lovingkindness: according unto the multitude of thy tender mercies blot out my transgressions.

Wash me thoroughly from mine iniquity, and cleanse me from my sin.

For I acknowledge my transgressions: and my sin is ever before me.

Purge me with hyssop, and I shall be clean: wash me, and I shall be whiter than snow.

Hide thy face from my sins, and blot out all mine iniquities.

Create in me a clean heart, O God; and renew a right spirit within me.

Restore unto me the joy of thy salvation; and uphold me with thy free spirit.

Then will I teach transgressors thy ways; and sinners shall be converted unto thee. — Psalm 51:1-3, 7, 9-10, 12-13.

Let us pray:

Almighty and most gracious God, our heavenly Father, who dost not deal with us after our sins nor rewardest us according to our iniquities: For Thy Name's sake, pardon our transgressions and cleanse us from all sin. Teach us through our illness to rely more on Thee than we trust in the help of man. Heal our soul's diseases that our body may be brought more readily back to health; we pray through our Lord Jesus Christ. Amen.

— 4 —

O Lord, thou hast searched me, and known me.

Thou knowest my downsitting and mine uprising, thou understandest my thought afar off.

Thou compassest my path and my lying down, and art acquainted with all my ways.

For there is not a word in my tongue, but, lo, O Lord, thou knowest it altogether.

Thou hast beset me behind and before, and laid thine hand upon me.

Search me, O God, and know my heart: try me, and know my thoughts:

And see if there be any wicked way in me, and lead me in the way everlasting. — Psalm 139:1-5, 23-24.

Let us pray:

O merciful and strong God, our heavenly Father, whose mercy is from everlasting to everlasting upon them that fear Thee: We bow in humble submission to Thy judgments, for Thy judgments are righteous altogether. We plead Thy help in accepting all Thy providences, for all things that Thou sendest us are for our good. Heal our backslidings, O merciful Father, and forgive us so that we may find comfort and peace now in our affliction and the blessed assurance that, even in our straying, Thou dost never leave us alone; we pray through Jesus Christ our Lord. Amen.

— 5 —

Come unto me, all ye that labour, and are heavy laden, and I will give you rest.

Take my yoke upon you, and learn of me; for I am meek and lowly in heart: and ye shall find rest unto your souls.

For my yoke is easy, and my burden is light.

If any man will come after me, let him deny himself, and take up his cross, and follow me.

For whosoever will save his life shall lose it: and whosoever will lose his life for my sake shall find it.

For what is a man profited, if he shall gain the whole world, and lose his own soul? — Matthew 11:28-30; 16:21-26.

Let us pray:

Almighty God, the Father of our Lord and Saviour Jesus Christ, who art a refuge for the weary, a shelter in time of trouble, and who will never forsake them that seek Thy face: We come to Thee in answer to Thy call to us. Teach us to be truly Thine own, trusting Thee in sickness or in health and in temptations strong; through Jesus Christ, who taught us when we pray to say:

Our Father which art in heaven, Hallowed be thy name.

Thy kingdom come. Thy will be done in earth, as it is in heaven.

Give us this day our daily bread.

And forgive us our debts, as we forgive our debtors.

And lead us not into temptation, but deliver us from evil: For thine is the kingdom, and the power, and the glory, for ever. Amen.

For the Aged

— 1 —

But though our outward man perish, yet the inward man is renewed day by day.

For our light affliction, which is but for a moment, worketh for us a far more exceeding and eternal weight of glory; While we look not at the things which are seen, but at the things which are not seen: for the things which are seen are temporal; but the things which are not seen are eternal.

And he said unto me, My grace is sufficient for thee: for my strength is made perfect in weakness. Most gladly therefore will I rather glory in my infirmities, that the power of Christ may rest upon me. — I Corinthians 4:16-18; 12:9.

Let us pray:

Almighty and all-wise God, our heavenly Father, in whom there is no changing, neither any shadow of turning: We thank Thee for Thy constant companionship that hath blessed our days and comforted us in our loneliness. Be Thou pleased, O merciful God, to keep our spirit strong and cheerful even though the weight of years and the infirmities of our body do encumber us. Our steps are slow; our strength is weak; our eyes are dim. But Thou, O Lord, orderest the steps of them that fear Thee; Thou makest their strength perfect in weakness; and Thou art eyes to those who cannot see. With childlike hearts, we entreat Thee, the God of our fathers and mothers, to walk with us as Thou hast done in the past and never leave us alone. In the evening of our day, give us light which streams from eternity, even Thy dwelling-place; we pray through Jesus Christ, our elder Brother. Amen.

— 2 —

Hast thou not known? hast thou not heard, that the everlasting God, the Lord, the Creator of the ends of the earth, fainteth not, neither is weary? there is no searching of his understanding.

He giveth power to the faint; and to them that have no might he increaseth strength.

Even the youths shall faint and be weary, and the young men shall utterly fall:

But they that wait upon the Lord shall renew their strength; they shall mount up with wings as eagles; they shall run, and not be weary; and they shall walk, and not faint. — Isaiah 40:28-31.

Let us pray:

All-wise and everlasting God, our heavenly Father, in whom our fathers and mothers before us trusted: Thou art our strength, our buckler and shield; Thou art our exceeding great reward. Grant that we may ever lean upon Thy strong arm when we feel our grip on life failing, and be Thou our daily support in the midst of the extremities of want and bodily weakness. Feed us with the Living Bread so that our spiritual strength is renewed, and give us the grace of patience to wait cheerfully and expectantly upon Thy welcome voice. We would commune with Thee, O heavenly Father, in a heavenly language, for we seek a city that hath foundations, even in that land where the wicked shall cease from troubling and the weary are at rest. Be Thou pleased to grant us Thy healing nearness and Thy Holy Spirit to guide us at last to a land of heavenly rest; through Jesus Christ our Lord. Amen.

— 3 —

Lord, thou hast been our dwelling place in all generations.

Before the mountains were brought forth, or ever thou hadst formed the earth and the world, even from everlasting to everlasting, thou art God.

O satisfy us early with thy mercy; that we may rejoice and be glad all our days.

Make us glad according to the days wherein thou hast afflicted us, and the years wherein we have seen evil.

Let thy work appear unto thy servants, and thy glory unto their children.

And let the beauty of the Lord our God be upon us. . . . Psalm 90:1-2, 14-17.

Let us pray:

Almighty and everlasting God, our heavenly Father, whose mercy and lovingkindness are known to all who trust in Thee: We thank Thee for Thy unfailing promises to us Thy children. Generation after generation seek Thee, and are found of Thee. We cast ourselves upon Thee, and are supported by Thee. We live secure in the sure and certain fulfillment of Thy precious promises. Thou hast promised, O God, that while the earth remaineth, seedtime and harvest, and cold and heat, and summer and winter, and day and night shall not cease. We praise Thy Name for these manifestations of Thy unfailing providence.

In the midst of sorrow or joy, sickness or health, adversity or prosperity, grant, we beseech Thee, that we may never lose sight of Thee. And when the storms of confusion and uncertainty overtake us, speak peace to our soul, O blessed Lord, and enlighten our mind with Thy Holy Spirit. Lighten our burdens by strengthening our spirit. Keep us strong and give us courage.

And when the ways of our common life would tend to discourage and to embitter us, give us the grace and the patience to maintain a loving and a confident spirit; through Jesus Christ our Lord. Amen.

For Those Who Have Recovered

— 1 —

Bless the Lord, O my soul: and all that is within me, bless his holy name.

Bless the Lord, O my soul, and forget not all his benefits:

Who forgiveth all thine iniquities; who healeth all thy diseases;

Who redeemeth thy life from destruction; who crowneth thee with lovingkindness and tender mercies;

Who satisfieth thy mouth with good things; so that thy youth is renewed like the eagle's.

Bless the Lord, all his works in all places of his dominion: bless the Lord, O my soul. — Psalm 103:1-5, 22.

Let us pray:

O God and Father of our Lord Jesus Christ: Blessed be Thy Name for healing all our diseases and saving our life from destruction. In our afflictions, Thou didst teach us patience and Thou didst draw us nearer to Thee. Teach us now, O heavenly Father, to speak of Thy glorious honor, Thy majesty and Thy marvelous works to us; through Jesus Christ our Lord. Amen.

— 2 —

I love the Lord, because he hath heard my voice and my supplications.

Because he hath inclined his ear unto me, therefore will I call upon him as long as I live.

The sorrows of death compassed me, and the pains of hell gat hold upon me: I found trouble and sorrow.

Then called I upon the name of the Lord; O Lord, I beseech thee, deliver my soul.

Gracious is the Lord, and righteous; yea, our God is merciful. — Psalm 116:1-5.

Let us pray:

We thank Thee, O gracious heavenly Father, for the preservation of our life. In times of danger, Thou didst watch over us, and in illness, Thou wast by our bed of pain. Thou didst lay Thy hand

upon us, and we were whole again. Bind our heart in loyalty to
Thee and let our life be lived in faithfulness to Thee; through
Jesus Christ our Lord. Amen.

— 3 —

I called upon thy name, O Lord, out of the low dungeon.

Thou hast heard my voice: hide not thine ear at my breathing,
at my cry.

Thou drewest near in the day that I called upon thee: thou
saidst, Fear not.

O Lord, thou hast pleaded the causes of my soul; thou hast redeemed my life. — Lamentations 3:55-58.

Let us pray:

O Lord our God: Thou hast spared us through many dangers
seen and unseen. When our affliction laid us low, Thine everlasting arms were there to hold us and to keep us from sinking into
despair. Thou didst lead us through the darkness of perplexity to
the light of utter trust in Thy faithfulness. Accept, we beseech
Thee, our sacrifice of praise and prayer; through Jesus Christ our
Lord. Amen.

— 4 —

The Lord preserveth the simple: I was brought low, and he
helped me.

Return unto thy rest, O my soul; for the Lord hath dealt
bountifully with thee.

For thou hast delivered my soul from death, mine eyes from
tears, and my feet from falling.

I will walk before the Lord in the land of the living.

What shall I render unto the Lord for all his benefits toward
me?

I will take the cup of salvation, and call upon the name of the
Lord. — Psalm 116:6-9, 12-13.

Let us pray:

O blessed Lord, our God and Father: We bless Thy Name for
Thy manifold blessings towards us. Thou hast taught us in temptation to trust only in Thy strength. When sorely tempted by pro-

tracted illness and pain to doubt Thy mercy and Thy love, Thou
didst draw near to us to lift us nearer to Thee. We praise Thee,
for Thou hast been mindful of us, and hast rescued us from peril,
sickness and temptation. Teach us always to remember Thy gifts of
grace to us; through Jesus Christ our Lord. Amen.

FOR THOSE WHO FACE DEATH

— 1 —

As the hart panteth after the water brooks, so panteth my soul
after thee, O God.

My soul thirsteth for God, for the living God: when shall I come
and appear before God?

Whom have I in heaven but thee? and there is none upon earth
that I desire beside thee.

My flesh and my heart faileth: but God is the strength of my
heart, and my portion for ever. — Psalm 42:1-2; 73:25-26.

Let us pray:

O Lord God, our ever blessed Father: We stretch out our hands
unto Thee, for our soul thirsteth after Thee, in a weary land. Come
speedily to our aid and satisfy our longing souls. Cause us to
know Thy lovingkindness in the morning and Thy tender mercies
every night. We lift up our soul unto Thee, and pray that Thy
goodness shall follow us unto the end; through Jesus Christ our
Lord. Amen.

— 2 —

For we know that if our earthly house of this tabernacle were
dissolved, we have a building of God, a house not made with
hands, eternal in the heavens.

Therefore we are always confident, knowing that, whilst we are
at home in the body, we are absent from the Lord:

We are confident, I say, and willing rather to be absent from
the body, and to be present with the Lord.

Wherefore we labour, that, whether present or absent, we may
be accepted of him. — II Corinthians 5:1, 6, 8-9.

Let us pray:

O eternal God, our heavenly Father, our refuge and strength for ever: Be Thou our unfailing help and sure defense when our earthly refuge and helpers fail. Shelter our soul when there is none other to protect us; preserve our soul from corruption. Attend unto our cry, O heavenly Father, and deliver us from fear and distrust; through Jesus Christ our Lord. Amen.

— 3 —

He that dwelleth in the secret place of the most High shall abide under the shadow of the Almighty.

I will say of the Lord, He is my refuge and my fortress: my God; in him will I trust.

Surely he shall deliver thee from the snare of the fowler, and from the noisome pestilence.

He shall cover thee with his feathers, and under his wings shalt thou trust: his truth shall be thy shield and buckler.

Thou shalt not be afraid for the terror by night; nor for the arrow that flieth by day;

Nor for the pestilence that walketh in darkness; nor for the destruction that wasteth at noonday. — Psalm 91:1-6.

Let us pray:

O Gracious God: We know that Thy mercy is in the heavens; that Thy faithfulness reaches unto the clouds; and that Thy judgments are very deep. Be Thou pleased, O Lord, to let Thy mercy reach down to us, and let Thy faithfulness quiet and comfort our spirit. Teach us a willing obedience to Thy judgments where we cannot understand, but grant that in Thy light, we may see light; through Jesus Christ our Lord. Amen.

ADMINISTRATION OF THE LORD'S SUPPER FOR THE SICK AND SHUT-IN

The celebration of The Lord's Supper in a home or hospital should be brief but reverent and unhurried. In a hospital, undue attention should not be drawn to this Service for the sake of the communicant as well as the other patients who are not involved.

Due regard should be had for the condition and comfort of the sick patient in the use of this Service.

Opening Sentences:

O taste and see that the Lord is good: blessed is the man that trusteth in him. — Psalm 34:8.

I am the bread of life [saith the Lord]: he that cometh to me shall never hunger; and he that believeth on me shall never thirst. — John 6:35.

Unto thee, O Lord, do I lift up my soul. O my God, I trust in thee. — Psalm 25:1-2.

Prayer of Preparation:

Our heavenly Father: Prepare our hearts for this feast and for communion with Thee as we offer thanks for our redemption through Thy Son, Jesus Christ, for the guidance we receive through Thy Church, the comfort we find through Thy Word and for the inspiration which comes to us as we remember the saints on earth and in heaven; for Jesus' sake. Amen.

Prayer of Consecration:

Hear the words of the Apostle Paul as we offer a prayer of consecration: Let a man examine himself, and so let him eat of that bread, and drink of that cup. — I Corinthians 11:28.

Let us pray:

Consecrate, we pray Thee, this bread and this wine for our spiritual use. And may we, through the Holy Spirit, be cleansed of all sin, drawn closer to Thee, and find our health in Thee, as we partake of these elements; through Jesus Christ our Lord. Amen.

Offering of the Bread:

Taking the Bread, the Minister shall say:

The Lord Jesus took bread, and when He had blessed it, He broke it *[the Minister breaks the Bread as he speaks]*, and gave it to His disciples, as I now give this bread to you in Christ's Name *[gives the Bread to the communicant]*. "Take, eat: this is my body, which is broken for you: do this in remembrance of me."

OFFERING OF THE WINE:

Pausing for a moment, the Minister offers the Wine, saying:
After the same manner our Lord took the cup *[the Minister takes the Wine],* and having given thanks, as I have done in His Name, He gave it to His disciples, as I now give it to you *[hands the Wine to the communicant],* saying, "This cup is the new testament in my blood: drink ye all of it."

CLOSING PRAYER:

After another brief pause, the Minister shall offer a closing prayer and the Benediction.

God be merciful unto us, and bless us, and cause His face to shine upon us; that Thy way may be known upon earth, Thy saving health among all nations. Amen.

BENEDICTION:

The peace of God, which passeth all understanding, keep your heart and your thoughts in Jesus Christ. Amen.

SECTION SEVEN

Prayers for Various Needs and Special Occasions

GUIDING PRINCIPLES AND PRACTICAL SUGGESTIONS

Non-liturgical Churches believe that prayer should be free and that this belief should be carefully defended and guarded. This does not mean, however, that liberty in prayer should become license or that prayer in the public worship of God should not be thoughtfully and appropriately considered and phrased.

The prayers appearing in this section for various needs and special occasions are meant to be instructive, suggestive and optional specimens. Their words or similar words may be used by the Minister. In these prayers are employed, as nearly as possible, the language of Scripture with which Christians are most familiar.

In order for public prayer to be meaningful to the worshiper and to evoke in him the deepest personal response of gratitude or praise, confession or need, petition or intercession, it must move from the general to the particular. Special mercies or graces and specific acts of God's goodness must be enumerated in public prayer to induce the worshiper to feel that he is deeply and personally involved in the prayer that is being uttered. Public prayer should give expression to the corporate and personal needs, aspirations and feelings, of the Congregation. Public prayer, through the Minister, should say for many worshipers what they cannot say for themselves but what they feel deep down in their hearts. It should deepen their sympathies, broaden their interests, unite them more firmly with the fellowship of faith and suffering, and expose them to an edifying power beyond calculation.

Let public prayer be free, but let it be thoughtful and appropriate, specific and meaningful, to the worshiper.

MORNING PRAYERS

— 1 —

O Lord our God, who hast prepared the light and the sun, and claimest both the night and the day: May our consciousness of Thee and of Thy bountiful care of all Thy children be awakened with the morning. As each new day brings with it new opportunities, help us courageously to face the old demands which we have thus far avoided, and diligently to perform the tasks which we have left undone. Grant unto us strength for the day and a renewal of spirit that we may rejoice and be glad in Thee. Let none whose spirits long for Thee be left unsatisfied. Let not those who wait for Thee be disappointed. And those who feel most alone this day, cause them to know that Thou thinkest of them, and art even with them. Grant that Thy children, wherever they may be, O God, may find this day a day of grace and blessing; we pray through Thy Son Jesus Christ. Amen.

— 2 —

Most merciful God, our Father, who scatterest the darkness so that there is light: We lift our hearts and our thoughts to Thee in a morning sacrifice. For we would begin the day with Thee. As Thou hast given the light of day to a waking world, be Thou pleased to grant light unto our minds to guide us through the devious paths we shall come upon this day. Help us to be wise in the decisions and selective in the choices we may be called upon to make. Direct our spirits, O God, that we may know where to find help and strength which no *man* can give us in the hour of deep and pressing need. Be Thou our strong God and Defender to protect and prosper our city; to bless and to guard our homes; to comfort the disconsolate; to strengthen the weak; and to encourage the strong. Be pleased to deliver us from all ignorance and sin, vain strivings, and all that is evil; so that we may come to the end of this day still with Thee; through Jesus Christ our Lord. Amen.

— 3 —

O God, we seek from Thee the preparation of our hearts for calling upon Thy name aright in this morning hour of worship.

The week just past has filled our hearts and minds with many things. Our spirits are weary and lift themselves to Thee but heavily. Sanctify and cleanse our thoughts. Relieve us of the strain and stress our souls have known through the many activities of daily living. Quiet our spirits, and speak peace to us that we may be receptive to Thy presence and receive the benefits of Thy Word; through Jesus Christ our Lord. Amen.

EVENING PRAYERS

— 1 —

Abide with us, O gracious heavenly Father, for it is toward evening and the day is far spent. We need Thy quiet, refreshing presence as we turn from the preoccupations and the stress and strain of the day. Our minds have been filled with many thoughts, and the cares that fill the day have left us little time for sober reflection or for many thoughts of Thee. The evening hour and withdrawal from a busy world reveal our emptiness and how little of value we garner from our multitude of activities of the day. We turn to Thee at eventide, O merciful God, unfilled and weary of mind and body. Fill our minds now with thoughts of Thee and our hearts with gratitude for the day's close and its promise of rest. Remember not against us our errors and the iniquities of the day. Cover our sins with Thy mercy. May the good intentions of our words and deeds and the inclination of our hearts toward integrity find favor in Thy sight as our record of the day is divinely judged; through Jesus Christ our Lord. Amen.

— 2 —

O Lord our God, open our eyes to see the glory of Thy heavens when in the evening hour we lift our eyes to Thee. Let Thy glory shine forth in the night as in the day; for the night and the day are the same to Thee. Cause the light of Thy glory to subdue the darkness of our minds as we meditate upon Thee and heed Thy voice through Thy Word. Grant that our lives may glorify Thee in a deeper reverence and an unfaltering trust in Thy mercies. Direct our thoughts in praise of Thee, and assist us when we pray.

Guard and protect us through our sleeping hours, and uphold our souls in life, if this be Thy holy will. But, if during the night, we sleep the sleep of death, be Thou present, O loving Father, to guide us to the shore of Thy eternal rest and the land of endless day; through Jesus Christ our Lord. Amen.

— 3 —

O merciful and holy Father, who slumberst not nor sleepest, but art watchful over Thy children: Be Thou our keeper when the day declineth and the night cometh upon us. Lift our hearts in praise to Thee this night for Thy watchful care over us, and for thoughts of Thee which are precious to us. Draw our spirits close to Thee, and let us feel Thy nearness to us when we call upon Thy Name; for the night shineth as the day when Thou art with us, and when we are in communion with Thee. O Thou who keepest us and watchest over us, preserve our souls through this night and protect us from all harm; through our Lord Jesus Christ. Amen.

PRAYERS OF THANKSGIVING
For God's Care and Leading

Our gracious heavenly Father, who sustainest Thy creation with wisdom, power and lovingkindness: We thank Thee that Thou hast not been unmindful of us. Thy holy loftiness has reached down to us in the loneliness of our erring ways through Thy Son Jesus Christ, that we may become conscious of the dignity we have in Thee, and that we may see the possibilities of our redemption and the renewal of our spirit through Thy grace. Thou makest Thy loving concern known to us in our weakness, in our sorrows, in our struggles and in our woes. We are confident in the midst of life's changes that Thou hast been our dwelling-place in all generations and our refuge in the time of trouble. When we doubt Thy nearness and ever present help, O gracious God, forgive our lack of faith, and lead us in those ways where, meeting and committing ourselves to Thee, we may lose our doubts and conquer our fears. When Thou speakest to us through adversity or fortune, through joy or pain, through peace or confusion, may we recognize Thy voice and listen. May we heed Thy voice, that our soul may find peace. When Thou seekest to guide us through hitherto unknown and untried ways, or even through the familiar paths, O heavenly Father, may we not counter Thy wisdom and Thy will for us with a proud and rebellious spirit. Teach us from our hearts to say: Thy will be done; through Jesus Christ our Lord. Amen.

For God's Wise and Gracious Gifts

Blessed art Thou, Lord God, whose providence is always wise and good, and whose care for Thy children is always bountiful. For bread and the food of companionship, we give Thee thanks. For strong hands and loyal hearts of friends and fellow workers; for words of encouragement and friendly advice; for rebuke when we are wrong and for the scrutinizing eye that makes us do our best; we thank Thee. Keep us ever grateful for the good Thou sendest us, whether in the guise of pleasure or of pain. Let us see Thy hand working for our good in life's bitters and its sweets that we may always rejoice in Thee, the God of our salvation and our hope for ever; through Jesus Christ our Lord. Amen.

For the Holy Word

We thank Thee, O gracious God, for Thy Holy Word upon which we feed and by which our feet are kept from straying. Thou dost give life to our souls and light to our minds. When our daily bread cannot sustain us, Thou upholdest our life with Thy Word. When human knowledge cannot make us wise where we need most to be wise, Thou dost illumine our minds with the light of Thy Holy Spirit. For the blessing of Thy Holy Word and Thy Holy Spirit to make clear Thy revelations to us, we thank and praise Thy name; through Jesus Christ our Lord. Amen.

PRAYERS OF CONFESSION
For Unfaithfulness

O God, our heavenly Father, Thou who seekest us when we stray from Thee. Forgive us for not desiring Thee as we ought. We have not always remembered Thy mercies in the day of prosperity. We have professed our knowledge of Thee, and yet we have denied Thee in our conduct and deeds. We acknowledge our unfaithfulness to Thee and our lack of zeal for Thy Kingdom's work. Help us, O God, to be truly repentant of our sins, and be Thou pleased to forgive us; through Jesus Christ our Lord. Amen.

For Impatience

Our life is filled with impatience, O Lord God. We fret and murmur under the necessity of waiting. We are impatient when we must trust Thee and Thee alone, when problems are not immediately solved or worries and cares removed at once. The difficulties of daily work and the necessity of routine grow too much for us. We are impatient with the cares of home, with the ignorance of those seeking to learn, with the slow growth of many seeking to be mature, even with the progress of Thy Church and Thy Kingdom. Teach us, O God, how to wait patiently for the things which require patience, and how to act with a holy impatience upon the things which require changing now; through Jesus Christ our Lord. Amen.

For Lack of Courage

We acknowledge that we are too easily turned from Thee and Thy Church, O merciful Father. We are not courageous enough to suffer for our convictions, nor even to stand publicly for them. We fear the loss of prestige and the fellowship of friends. We have sacrificed our individual differences in order to conform to the crowd. Hence we have lost ourselves. Help us, O gracious God, to find ourselves by truly finding Thee; we pray through Jesus Christ our Lord. Amen.

For Ignorance

We pray, O gracious God, to be delivered from ignorance, which is the lack of knowledge of Thy Word. We have not attended to the ministry of Thy Word; nor have we sought the knowledge required of children of light. Our ignorance of Thee and Thy Word has led us into shame, and sometimes into evil. We have been led to make bad decisions and often to act rashly and unwisely. Our lack of knowledge and wisdom has sometimes made cowards of us. But Thou, O Lord God, canst deliver us from ignorance and cowardice by the gracious indwelling of Thy Holy Spirit. Help us to humble ourselves before Thee, and inspire us to a diligent study of Thy Word and to an openness of mind and heart to receive it; through Jesus Christ our Lord. Amen.

PRAYERS OF PETITION

FOR A BETTER ATTITUDE AND SPIRIT TOWARD ALL PERSONS

O Thou, who art the maker of us all and didst give Thine only begotten Son for the redemption of the world Thou hast created: We plead for the will and the power to serve Thee as Thy children and to behave toward each other as brothers. Thou has made us all; teach us, O heavenly Father, to regard each other's dignity and worth, each other's individual differences and lawful interests. Save us from intolerance and bigotry, ill-will and disdain of a fellow human being. Teach us to understand each other as children of one heavenly Father and fellow creatures whose times are appointed and whose boundaries are set. May we grant to all others the understanding and patience, the esteem and fellow feeling we desire for ourselves; through Jesus Christ our Lord. Amen.

FOR MEN AND WOMEN OF GOOD WILL

For men and women of good will of all racial groups, in all geographical areas of our land, we pray, O God. Bless and preserve them to be the true and durable fabric of our national life. Give them an inexhaustible courage and patient continuance to support what is just and true. Grant unto them courageous faith in the essential decency of all, even when the conduct of others burdens this faith. Sustain them, O God, with a taste of the power of the world to come and evidences of the reality of Thy kingdom on earth; we pray through our Lord Jesus Christ. Amen.

For Inward Power

O merciful and strong God, who alone art faithful and true: Thou knowest that we need Thee when tempted and tried by the ills of life. Thou knowest how easily we give up hope and doubt Thy love for us when storms arise. Thou knowest that our heart may be turned from Thee as well as toward Thee when sorrows press our soul. Be merciful unto us, O God, and be Thou patient with us, for in our turning toward Thee or away from Thee, Thou knowest that we need Thee. Our own soul cries out to Thee in returning or in straying. We plead in the midst of the ills of life for the manifestation of Thy overruling power. Overrule the ills which we cannot avoid so that, though walking through the valley of the shadow of death, we may fear no evil. Let Thy Holy Spirit be in us the inward power of strength which subdues all our doubts and fears; through Jesus Christ our Lord and Master. Amen.

For Aid in Temptation

Almighty God, who art good to all and whose tender mercies are over all Thy works: We beseech Thee to grant unto us Thy mercy and Thy help in our struggle with temptation. We are not wise enough to know all the forms temptations may take; for we are tempted in prosperity as well as in the day of adversity. Our friends and our successes may become a temptation to us, as well as our enemies and our failures. The very strengths and abilities with which Thou hast endowed us may tempt us more gravely than our weaknesses and inadequacies. Prepare us for temptation, O God, and preserve us day by day with the presence of Thy Holy Spirit to enlighten our mind, to guide our steps, and to strengthen us in the inner man; through Jesus Christ our Lord. Amen.

For Faithfulness in Christian Work

Give to us, O heavenly Father, a creative spirit to do our common, often unexciting tasks, in uncommon, growth-inspiring ways. Equip us with an inexhaustible patience to sustain us through the long reaches of time from one point of progress to the next. Grant unto us the mood of praise and the spirit of gratitude to match our privilege of being entrusted with the service in which we are engaged. Rededicate us to the work and the faith to which we have committed ourselves, and may we never suffer any breach between our ideals and conduct. Reinforce our duty with loyalty. Lift it to the high place of a Christian calling, rooted in Thy will and inspired by the life of our Lord. Grant that we may be discontented with an inadequate performance of our tasks or the momentary fulfillment of our mission. May we be faithful unto death; through Jesus Christ our Lord. Amen.

To Confirm, Strengthen, and Encourage Workers

Grant us Thy love, O gracious heavenly Father, that we may overcome our impatience with the seeming slow results of the redemptive work in which we are engaged; that we may not grow impatient in our work against the ignorance or prejudices of our friends, our enemies, or our fellow workers. Help us to be militant without being unkind, uncompromising without being intolerant, devoted without being bigoted. Strengthen and embolden our spirits, O God who art power, that it will be no longer we who are holding on to Thee, but Thou who hast seized and possessed us; that we shall be no longer unsteady in our faith or unsure of the end-result of the work we undertake; through Jesus Christ our Lord. Amen.

For Holy Ambitions and Pure Motives

O God, we pray for a heart and mind to serve Thee worthily and for a life to shine with holy ambitions and pure motives. Save us from serving Thee to be seen of men, and from praying to be heard for our eloquence. Be Thou pleased to cleanse the thoughts of our mind and sanctify our heart that our inward ambitions and private motives may be openly expressed and publicly honored and supported. Draw us nearer to Thee so that, when we speak, our heart may not be far from Thee and what we purpose in our heart may be acceptable unto Thee; through Jesus Christ our Lord. Amen.

For a Humble, Obedient Spirit

Grant, O gracious God, our Father, that we may desire to know Thy thoughts and to fulfill Thy purposes. Take from us all wilful

pride that we may not have a rebellious spirit but may bend our
will to Thine. Help us to attain unto Thy holy and loving will
by desiring to will that which we hear from Thee. Whither thou
leadest us, may we trust Thee enough to follow. Whatsoever Thou
wouldst have us do, may we be faithful enough to do it. Let Thy
purposes and Thy will become ours; through Jesus Christ our
Lord. Amen.

For Temperance

Almighty God, who art wise in all Thy ways and art known to
all for the constancy of Thy ways to men: Grant us the grace to
be sober in thought and conduct. Temper our thoughts with Thy
wisdom and subdue our rebellious spirits with the constraining
power of Thy love. Keep us from all excesses, and bless our lives
with health and holiness, that we may be found acceptable to Thee
and an example of Thy keeping power; through Jesus Christ our
Lord. Amen.

For Making Wise Decisions

O God, give us the wisdom and courage to make wise decisions
and then to act upon them. Let us not be a hindrance to Thy
work because we fear making decisions or because we do not have
the courage to act upon the decisions we may make. Forgive us
when we err in judgment, O God, but let us not be afraid to make
honest mistakes. We know infinite wisdom belongeth only to Thee
and our best knowledge is but a reflection of Thy truth. May we
never refuse to make decisions that must be made, and may we
never refuse to act when action is demanded of us because we do
not have perfect knowledge. We plead for the action of Thy Holy
Spirit upon all we think and do. When we think and act according
to Thy will, O God, may Thy Spirit work through and in us.
When, in our thoughts and deeds, we forget Thee, then let Thy
Spirit work over us, and in spite of us. May Thy mind and Thy
work ultimately prevail; through Jesus Christ our Lord. Amen.

PRAYERS FOR SPECIAL USE
For the Church

Bless, O Lord God, the Church which Thou hast founded upon

the Rock, Christ our Lord. Arise and have mercy on Zion; for the time has come to favor her. Extend her borders through the spread of the Gospel and the salvation of many souls in many lands. Deepen the faith and loyalty of those who love her walls, that nothing may shake her foundation nor the gates of hell prevail against her. Let the fellowship of faith be bound together in a fellowship of love and strengthened by the unity of the Spirit in the bond of peace. Edify and equip Thy Church, O merciful Father, with Thy Word of truth, even the Holy Spirit, that Thy people may be confirmed in the faith, comforted by Thy grace, and encouraged by the expectation and manifestation of Thy glory; through Jesus Christ our Lord. Amen.

UNITY OF THE CHURCH

Almighty God, our heavenly Father, who hast loved the Church and given Thyself for her through Thy Son Jesus Christ: Be Thou pleased to sanctify and uphold her by Thy Word. Where she is weak, strengthen her; where she is defenseless, defend her; when she is corrupt, we beseech Thee, purge and cleanse her; when she is in error, correct and guide her. Heal her breaches, O God, and suffer no divisions to keep her permanently divided in faith, work, or in fellowship. Save her from needless divisions and preserve her from rivalry, bigotry, and an uncharitable spirit toward her many members. Teach us how to live in unity and peace, bearing with one another where we differ, and bring us into a closer, deeper fellowship with Thee; through Jesus Christ our Lord. Amen.

FOR CHRISTIAN MISSIONS

Almighty and everlasting God, our heavenly Father, who through Thy Son hast commissioned Thy Church to spread the Gospel to all nations, to teach them and to build them up into a fellowship worthy of Thy Name: Bless Thy Church with a missionary zeal to spread the Gospel at home and abroad. Open our eyes to see our missionary opportunities where we are and to recognize the whole world as our mission field. May our Church send missionaries from our land to other lands, not because our missionary task here is done, but because we would be obedient to Thy command and grateful to Thee for having prospered our country with resources enough to share with other peoples. Grant that the Holy Spirit may accompany and abide with those faithful and self-forgetful workers who have answered the call of missionary service. May our prayers, our gifts and our financial support contribute to the strength and faith by which they are sustained. Bless the Mission Board through which our support and efforts are channeled. Keep them wise and efficient in their administration, hopeful and confident of a greater response from our churches and greater results through the Holy Spirit on our mission fields. Keep us, O God, a Missionary Church, filled with Thy zeal, challenged by the Kingdom's goal and inspired by the Christian testimony of many souls from many lands; through Jesus Christ our Lord. Amen.

For the Distressed in Body and Mind

We are often brought into situations, O gracious God, which deny entrance to all but Thee and Thee alone. We are faced with circumstances which can be changed only at Thy behest. In such hard times for us, O heavenly Father, grant unto us the nearness of Thy presence and the blessing of Thy unfailing help. Uphold our soul in life. Let Thy light shine upon us when we are imprisoned in darkness. Guide our spirit when the light of our mind flickers and burns low. And calm the tempest that rages within us and about us; through Jesus Christ our Lord. Amen.

For Those Who Travel

For those whose pursuits take them far from home, we pray, O God. Direct their path, for only Thou canst make us to dwell in safety. On land or sea or in the air, protect them with Thy powerful hand and let Thine everlasting arms rest underneath them. Help them not to be afraid of the unknown or the future; but grant unto them the blessed assurance that our times are in Thy hands. May they, in faith and trust, leave them there with Thee. Guard and protect the home and family they leave behind. Keep them safe from all danger and fear. Be Thou pleased to keep them all joined in heart while they are apart, and bring them safely together again, if this be Thy will; through Jesus Christ our Lord. Amen.

FOR A COLLEGE COMMENCEMENT

Almighty and everlasting God, our heavenly Father, who hast called us to be children of light that we may be light to those who sit in the darkness of fear, ignorance and lethargy: We thank Thee that through Thy grace we have been brought to this day of commencement for these students who have been subjected to the discipline of this institution and exposed to its cultural heritage during the full course of their study and stay here. On this day of solemn jubilation for them, help them to know that they have learned much, but that there is much they have not learned. Teach them that the discipline of the mind and spirit and the maturity of the person are continuing processes; that though they leave this institution, they can never leave the school of life. In the midst of their life and work beyond these walls, grant that they may never need to feel too keenly the things they neglected to learn here or the things they should have done here but did not do. May they not be penalized for this miscalculation of the young, inexperienced mind. Let Thy presence go with them, and may they keep the knowledge and experience they have gained here alive and useful. Make them truly Thy servants in whatever pursuits they have chosen to follow. Give them an ever inquiring mind, the heart of a humanitarian and the lively interest of a responsible citizen in the community in which they will be established.

Bless now, we would pray Thee, O God, all higher institutions of learning, their administrators and faculties. Bless them with adequate resources to be effective in the discharge of their responsibility to the student, the nation and to Thee. Raise up friends for them, even donors to support their efforts and to further their visions. And be Thou, O God, the glory of all that they do, working in and through them Thy will for the people whom Thou hast created for Thyself and Thy glory; through Jesus Christ our Lord. Amen.

FOR PUBLIC EDUCATION

Almighty God, our heavenly Father, from whom all right pur-

poses and true judgments proceed, and in whose wisdom Thy
people become wise: We thank Thee for the establishment of the
system of public education in our land. Thou didst put it into the
minds of our fathers to insure our appreciation of the democratic
ideal to which our nation is committed, the preservation and development of the democratic processes by which we seek to
achieve our community and national goals, and the protection and
exercise of our civil rights and liberties, with the institution and
provision of public education for all the children of our citizenry.

We have not been awake as we should have been to the responsibility resting upon us, citizens and parents alike, to safeguard and
to support this system with a clearer understanding of its values and
present needs, with active concern and good will for its continuance and enlargement, with participation in the processes to which
we are competent to make a contribution, and with our financial
support of the school needs of our community and nation.

We have not sufficiently honored or valued the teaching profession so that our children are inspired to pursue it as a career or
our teachers encouraged in an ever deepening devotion to it.

Grant us, O merciful Father, willing and determined minds to
serve our children by making adequate provisions for their school
needs; to honor and stabilize our teaching profession by placing
a high estimate upon it as an indispensable instrument in achiev-
ing the goals of our way of life; to support this truly democratic
system by electing to office local board members of vision, courage
and a sense of what is first-rate in public education. But in all, O
gracious God, be Thou our guide, the source of all our aspirations,
and the stimulus of our efforts to keep central in our public education the importance of moral and spiritual values; we pray for the
sake of Thy Kingdom on earth. Amen.

For Christian Services Organization Assembly

Almighty God, our heavenly Father, whose gift in Thy Son to the
world awakens in us our own best potential and possibilities: Make
us in this assembly deeply conscious of Thee, and of the gifts with
which we have been endowed. Make us aware of the enormous
opportunities we have been granted in our generation, and chal-

lenge us with the wide influence we enjoy. Make us to know that
Thou, our Creator and Redeemer, dost hold each one of us to
account for the use of all our strengths and abilities, our powers
and privileges, our influence and opportunities. Remind us that
much is expected from those who have been given much. We
pray, O God, for Thy assistance to know what things are required
of us by Thee and by our fellow man. Help us to face the serious
facts of our times and to find in Thee our courage to meet them
with wisdom, discipline and resourcefulness.

Free us from all unworthy interests, false choices and the
frivolous mood in which our commitments to democratic and
Christian ideals are so often made. Release within us the power
of Thy Spirit with which a truly democratic and Christian nation
is obtainable now. Be pleased now, O gracious God, to grant to all
of us in these disturbing but tremendously hopeful times an un-
diminishing faith in the absolute necessity of an inward life, in the
efficacy of dedicated intelligence and in the power of an active,
even sacrificial, good will, that we may live today the life of a
better tomorrow; we would pray through Jesus Christ our Lord.
Amen.

For Community-Serving Organizations and Agencies

We pray, O God, for those organizations and agencies which, by
their ethical radicalism, have charted a course for themselves
through these turbulent and sometimes disheartening years, a
course that has kept them both loyal to their country and faithful
in their pursuit of the highest ideals of democracy. Grant that the
sleepers may be awakened to their stake in the struggle being
waged for them, that they may rally financially and morally to
the support of those great forces in our national life. Help them
to know that the ignorant and lazy, the indifferent and the dif-
fident, as well as the prejudiced, are not free; through Jesus Christ
our Lord. Amen.

For Interfaith Community Service

O God, grant unto us to know and to appreciate the privilege
which is ours to dedicate and to contribute the power of our mind
and spirit to the constructive and redemptive forces at work in our

common life; that we may seek Thy guidance in all our worthy pursuits and ever widening opportunities for a continuing service to Thee and to each other. May the deeper currents of faith and service, courage and sacrifice, be a power within us to do the things we ought, and to extend the boundaries of a full and enlightened life to all; this our common prayer, we pray. Amen.

FOR INTERFAITH SERVICES ASSEMBLY

Almighty God, who hast bound us all in a common toil and a common necessity: Grant that our hearts may be knit together in a common purpose and a common goal: a more just and equitable order and life for all. With clear minds, strong bodies, and determined effort may we strive and contend, without bitterness, for the things which issue in an abundant life for all Thy people. Grant that we may esteem the worth of men above the things which their strength and toil can produce, and may their labor bring them rewards and an enjoyment which shall insure for them a life worthy of Thy highest creation. Deliver us from all strife and selfishness, faint-heartedness and greed. Grant to us full and continuous employment and relief from anxiety. And may Thy Spirit give direction to all the deliberations of this body; this is our common prayer. Amen.

FOR THE COMMON (CITY) COUNCIL

Almighty and eternal God, who hast made known to us through Thy Son, Jesus Christ, Thy loving, yet critical, concern for the government, the institutions and the relationships of men: Grant, as we pause in this moment hallowed to Thee, that the spirit of prayer and reverence for Thy Name may prevail in these deliberations and that this council may be blessed with Thy aid. We pray that their affections may be guided by whatsoever things are true and honest, just and pure, lovely and of a good report; that their understandings may be enlightened by Thy wisdom; and that their spirits may be empowered by Thy Spirit. So sanctify their thoughts and intentions, their words and actions, that all they think or speak or do may redound to Thy honor and the well being of our municipality; we pray through Him who is our Lord and Master. Amen.

FOR A LEGISLATIVE ASSEMBLY

Almighty God, who hast granted unto this nation the democratic ideal by which our destiny may be fashioned: We thank Thee that Thou hast blessed our land to survive the infectious climate of confusion and uncertainty, helplessness and irresponsibility, by preserving among us enlightened and concerned citizens who cherish their heritage and who have purposed in their hearts to extend it. We thank Thee for like-minded leaders whom Thou hast raised up to guide our republic. We would pray that Thou wouldst grant those whom we have entrusted with the authority of government to be responsible and wise, courageous and strong. And guide us, the people, to expect of them and to support them in all wise legislation and a faithful administration that we may all prosper under an equal law. Defend our liberties and grant us a sense of our responsibility. Achieve unity of purpose among us, and grant unto us the victory of faith in the ideals to which we are committed as a nation. Strengthen us with honor and grant us peace. Provide us, O God, with the strength and spiritual sustenance for performing with might the tasks with which our common life yet confronts us; this is our common prayer. Amen.

PRAYERS FOR SPECIAL DAYS
FOR NEW YEAR'S DAY

O eternal and unchanging God, our heavenly Father: We thank Thee that it is by Thy grace that we have been brought to the beginning of this New Year. Let Thy mercies of old and Thy providence experienced through the past year teach us to leave all things in the coming year in Thy hands. The unknown future we face, and the stubborn difficulties through which we have already come, cause us to acknowledge our ignorance and our weakness. Grant that we may rely upon Thy wisdom and strength. Save us, O merciful Father, from unreal fears and premature worries; save us from fear and worry altogether. Give us committed hearts to Thee that, whatever our lot in the New Year, we may accept it courageously, confidently and quietly. For we know, O Lord God, that the dark days must come; that we are not exempt from sickness or trouble, pain or death. We only plead that Thou wilt keep us prepared to face these things without fear or distress, without complaint and lack of faith in Thy everlasting goodness. Preserve us through this year if it be Thy will. But if not, teach us from our heart to say: Thy will be done; through Jesus Christ our Lord. Amen.

FOR RACE RELATIONS SUNDAY

O God, by whom the dignity of man has been wondrously established, and by whom the duty of being free has been laid upon us: We pay homage to Thee and acknowledge our dependence upon Thee. For it is Thou, O Lord, who hast led us thus far on our way. Through events and through strong and patient men, Thou hast been firmly and unequivocally establishing the dignity and freedom of all men as a growing reality in a growing new world. We thank Thee, O God, for men and women who have hazarded their lives in the cause of human dignity and justice that both the victims and the conveyors of prejudice and hatred may be free. Thou hast blessed us with inspiring and challenging examples of such men and women, even in our midst. May they be continually nerved by Thee and supported by a growing host of men and women for whom freedom and justice have become imperatives; through Jesus Christ our Lord. Amen.

FOR EASTER SUNDAY

O merciful and redeeming God, our Father, who by the power of Thy Spirit hast transformed Easter into the Resurrection day of our Lord and Saviour Jesus Christ: Preserve in us and through us this day as a holy day. May we observe it with deep reverence and unbounded gratitude, for through Thy acts this day Thou hast secured for us the salvation of our souls, the resurrection of our bodies and the life everlasting. May it please Thee, O gracious God, to hold our lives in hope and faithfulness to Thy Son, through the Holy Spirit, until our Lord's return, when our bodies shall be raised incorruptible to meet Him and the Church Triumphant; through Jesus Christ our Lord. Amen.

For Memorial Day

Almighty God, who art the First and the Last, and who, in Thy Son, art the first fruit of them that sleep: We thank Thee for the glorious inspiration we have received and the blessed ties that bind us to the world unseen through our beloved dead. Their deeds of love and mercy live in us. Their valor and courage, their vision and sacrifice are our heritage. We bless their memory and pray that Thou wilt bless us, O Lord God, for their sake. Hold us in communion with them, and keep them alive in the work we do and in the tasks we have inherited from them. May we bring no dishonor upon their names or the work that they have entrusted to us. Be Thou pleased, Almighty God, to strengthen our hand, ennoble our spirit, and embolden us for any dangerous task to which we may be called. Grant through Thy grace that it may be said of us, the living, that we too died in faith, not having received all the promises, but having seen them afar off; we pray through Jesus Christ our Lord. Amen.

For Independence Day

Almighty God, who hast given this land to be a heritage to all the inhabitants of it: Make us gratefully conscious of our indebtedness to Thee — our Maker and Defender — and to the pioneering builders of a free land. Assembled here under the challenge of a Declaration of Independence not yet fully realized, do Thou deepen our appreciation of the worth of our common heritage. Give us the zeal fully to possess it and the wisdom and courage to safeguard it. Direct our efforts to achieve full freedom under an equal law for all our citizens, and make us one people in the desire and willing struggle for a nation indivisible under Thy governance. Give to our nation wise and fearless citizens to defend our liberties and to preserve for us a land of order and peace, of unity and strength, and of faith and righteousness. Guide and encourage us through rightly purposed pursuits to earn Thy favor and a worthy, responsible life for all; which is our common prayer. Amen.

For Labor Day

O gracious and eternal God, our heavenly Father, upon whom all Thy children do wait: Be Thou pleased to grant unto us our daily bread. It is Thou, O God, who openest Thy hand and satisfiest every living thing. Thou hast commanded us, Thy children, to subdue the earth and to earn our bread by the sweat of our brow; and Thou hast crowned us with wisdom and knowledge and provided us with strength for toil. Sanctify our strength and skills that they may be employed in a divine service, even the welfare of our fellow man. Into whatever position of responsibility our training and advantage may bring us, grant that we may be led by Thy Spirit to desire and to serve the common good. Whether in management or labor, grant that we may possess a Christian understanding of work and responsibility. Give also to us a sense of Christian vocation in whatever work we engage so that our country may prosper materially and the spiritual health of our nation be assured; through Jesus Christ our Lord. Amen.

For Church Loyalty (Rally) Sunday

Almighty God our heavenly Father, who didst in olden times raise up a people for Thy name, who through Thy Son didst redeem the world and establish the Church, and who by the Holy Spirit dost sustain, edify and renew it: Be thou pleased to glorify the Church through us. Make our daily lives a testimony of Thy keeping power. Grant that our loyalty to the Church and our support of its life and work may be abundantly evident. Increase our love for Thee and the Church which Thou lovest, so that we may willingly serve it and sacrifice for it as Thou through Thy Son hast done and continuest to do through the Holy Spirit. May we offer dedicated bodies and minds to Thy holy cause and a generous portion of our material substance to Thy work through the Church; through Jesus Christ our Lord, we pray. Amen.

For Christian Education Sunday

Most merciful and eternal God, who dost illumine all hearts and minds that seek Thee with Thy Word through the Holy Spirit: Increase our desire for knowledge of Thee that we may continually seek after it. Broaden our vision to see Thee wherever truth is found. Deepen our conviction to recognize all discovered truth as proceeding from Thy life and as a manifestation of Thy love and wisdom and power. Embolden us to stamp Thy Name on all the knowledge we may possess, that men may know that our highest knowledge is of Thee and our ultimate allegiance is to Thy Word. Bless, we would pray Thee, all teachers of Thy Holy Word. Grant that they may be disciples of Thy wisdom and living epistles of the Christian way of life. May the seeker and the learner both be given grace sufficient to their needs that those who seek Thee may find Thee, and those who would learn of Thee may find their yoke easy and their burden light. Keep Thy Church, O God, ever zealous and competent to teach Thy Word and to make many disciples for Thee; through Jesus Christ our Lord. Amen.

For United Nations Day

God of the nations and Saviour of the world, who inhabitest eternity and dwellest with him who is crushed: Grant unto us grateful hearts for persistent and enduring forces that make for righteousness and peace in our common life and for the opportunities and privileges we have to cooperate with them. In humble gratitude we memorialize all those of every race and nation and in every walk of life who have hazarded, even sacrificed, their life for the cause of peace and justice for all. Grant that we may follow their noble example, being dedicated to the highest and fullest possible life for all Thy people. We further pray that we may be granted singleness of purpose in our common tasks, sincerity of effort, and an insatiable desire for peace and good will among men; through Jesus Christ our Lord. Amen.

For Reformation Sunday

O Thou whose faithfulness is without end and who desirest faithfulness of Thy people to Thee: We thank Thee for the faithful in every generation who have been true to their covenant with Thee; who have been unashamed in their profession of faith, dependable in the exercise of their Christian duty, and courageous in contending for the faith which once for all times has been delivered to the saints. Thou didst preserve some in times of danger when their companions fell, and Thou didst watch over others when no one cared but Thee. Thou didst make them all victorious over the world and conquerors of doubt and the fear of death itself.

May it please Thee, O heavenly Father, to have mercy upon us who have not faithfully followed Thy Word or honored the goodly heritage to which we, by Thy grace, have become heirs. Arouse the negligent among us, strengthen those who are weak in the faith, embolden those who do not publicly own Thy Name or contend for a New Testament faith. Enlighten those who are perplexed in faith; and give to all who are content only to please Thee, the victory of faith; through our Lord Jesus Christ. Amen.

FOR THANKSGIVING DAY

We praise Thee, O God, for Thy lovingkindness in the morning and Thy faithfulness every night. Thou art good to us, and Thy mercies are over all Thy works. We wait upon Thee, and Thou, O Lord, givest us our meat in due season. Day after day, Thou providest for our needs. Thou openest Thy hand and satisfiest the desire of every living thing. We thank Thee for the world which Thou hast created, for the work it demands of us, and its beauty surrounding us. Thou Thyself art the glory of the day and of the night. Thou givest to us summer and winter, seedtime and harvest, cold and heat. Thy words are unsearchable and Thy mercies without end. We thank and praise Thee for the land of our birth where freedom is precious and worship is free. Although our land has been afflicted many times by the dark counsels of hate and irreligion, yet Thy name is feared and law and order prevail. For opportunities of work and education, we bless Thy Name, O Most High. Thou hast ordained that man should labor and earn his bread by the sweat of his brow; that he should scorn idleness and ignorance. For those who do Thy will both in providing jobs for us and in training our minds and hands for useful work and profitable leisure, we praise Thy Holy Name.

We praise and honor Thee for the place we call home. Humble or pretentious, Thou shelterest it with Thy loving care. We thank

Thee for its family ties, its refuge from the crowd, and its patient and suffering love. Thou art the protection of each home and the rest and the ground of family reverence. For the multitude of Thy mercies towards us, let all Thy works praise Thee; and may Thy people ever bless Thee; through Jesus Christ our Lord. Amen.

For Universal Bible Sunday

Eternal and wise God, our heavenly Father, by whose Word the heavens and the earth were created: We thank Thee that Thy Word through us hath not been spoken in vain. Thou hast sent it forth in the power of the Holy Spirit and hast blessed it to be planted and rooted in many hearts in many lands. We thank Thee that through the unheralded labors and sacrifices of many of Thy faithful servants — scholars and teachers, messengers and missionaries — Thy Word has been made available through the printed page in many lands. Grant, O God, that those who possess and read the Bible may see beyond the printed page to the Living Word which Thou dost speak to us here and now, as Thou hast spoken in every generation to them who have had an ear to hear. Give power to Thy Holy Word that the unsaved may be reached and drawn to Thee and that the saved may be established, strengthened, comforted and encouraged; through Jesus Christ our Lord. Amen.

For Christmas Day

O gracious heavenly Father: We thank Thee that through Thy tender mercy the dayspring from on high hath visited us to give light to them that sit in darkness and in the shadow of death and to guide our feet into the way of peace. Grant that we, and all the ends of the earth, may this day look to Thee for our salvation; for Thou alone art the ruler of the world and the source of all things that endure. Help us this day to commit ourselves to Thee and to seek those things that are above. As we face the cares and the temptations that fill each day, grant to us the moral courage and strength to abide the day of distress and to resist evil. May we not be ashamed or afraid to take our stand with righteousness, justice and truth. Help us, through dedicated and courageous personal living, to testify to the advent of Thy Son into the world, and into our hearts, that His life may be the light of all who would seek His face. Use us, O God, for the achievement of peace and understanding in our world. Use us, by helping us to be victorious in the little things that fret and tempt us. Let no job seem too small for us to do well; no decision too unimportant in which to seek Thy guidance; no human being too insignificant to be treated as a person. Use us, our heavenly Father, to Thy honor and Thy glory this day; through Jesus Christ our Lord. Amen.

A Year of Scripture Readings

LECTIONARY FOR THE CHURCH YEAR

Based on the Main Themes and Days of the Church Year and the Civil Calendar, with alternate selections for optional use.

This lectionary provides for Responsive Readings from the Psalter and lessons from the Old and New Testaments for morning and evening. Alternate Scripture selections are given for each Sunday for morning and evening. The combination in which these lections are employed is left to the discretion of the user.

A four-week month is used as the basis of this lectionary in order to designate the stationary special days of the Church Year and those of the Civil Year which are generally observed. The movable days are provided for in a separate lectionary from which the user is expected to select appropriate lections for these special movable days as well as for undesignated fifth Sundays and that most rare fifty-third Sunday in the year.

JANUARY

	PSALTER*		OLD TESTAMENT		NEW TESTAMENT	
	MORNING OR EVENING	MORNING	EVENING	MORNING	EVENING
1st Sunday (New Year's Sunday)	96, 138, 90, 91	Deuteronomy 6:1-13 Isaiah 65:17-25	Joshua 3 Isaiah 2	Revelation 1:4, 6-8, 18 Matthew 6:25-34	Revelation 21:1-7 Matthew 7:21-27
2d Sunday (First Sunday after Epiphany)	100, 72 46, 97	Isaiah 60:1-5, 18-22 Micah 4:1-5; 5:2-4	Isaiah 19:19-25 Isaiah 45:1-7	Matthew 2:1-12 Luke 2:21-40	Matthew 2:12-23 Luke 2:41-52
3d Sunday	65, 84 66, 122	Ruth 1 Jonah 3:1-4:2	Isaiah 45:8-14 Isaiah 45:15-19	Matthew 25:1-13 Colossians 1:21-29	Colossians 1:1-20 II Peter 1
4th Sunday (Youth Sunday, Last Sunday in January)	67, 92 85, 93	Isaiah 5 Proverbs 1:7-23	Isaiah 45:20-25 Ezekiel 11:14-21	I Corinthians 2:6-16 II Corinthians 4:1-6	Ephesians 3 I Corinthians 2

*Responsive reading

197

FEBRUARY

| | PSALTER* | OLD TESTAMENT | | NEW TESTAMENT | |
	MORNING OR EVENING	MORNING	EVENING	MORNING	EVENING
1st Sunday	92, 117 95, 118	Proverbs 3:1-26 Genesis 41:14-39	Proverbs 2:3-9 I Kings 3:5-14	Luke 10:25-27 John 4:1-42	I John 2:8-17 John 3:1-17
2d Sunday (Race Relations Sunday)	98, 114 8, 131	Leviticus 19:1-4, 9-15 Hosea 11:1-9	Genesis 1:1-19 Hosea 6:1-6	Matthew 4:1-11 James 1	Luke 4:16-30 Ephesians 6:10-17
3d Sunday (Brother- hood Sunday)	41, 139 15, 133	Exodus 3:1-15 Amos 6:1-6	Genesis 2:4-9, 15-25 Zechariah 7:8-14	Romans 8:12-39 Romans 14	Luke 14:26-33 I Peter 2:11-16
4th Sunday	51, 39 19 79:8-13	Genesis 3 Genesis 28:10-22	Joel 2:12-18 Jonah 2	Romans 7 Luke 13:24-30	Romans 8:1-11 Hebrews 10:21-31

*Responsive reading

198

MARCH

| | PSALTER* | OLD TESTAMENT | | NEW TESTAMENT | |
	MORNING OR EVENING	MORNING	EVENING	MORNING	EVENING
1st Sunday	1, 130 24, 115	Exodus 20:1-20 Isaiah 1:2-20	Micah 6:1-8 Micah 7:1-9	Matthew 5:1-20 Matthew 22:34-40	Matthew 5:21-48 Romans 12:1-21
2d Sunday	26, 85 27, 42	Isaiah 56:1-8 Ezekiel 18:20-23, 31-32	Nahum 1:3-7 Habakkuk 1:1-4, 12-13a	Matthew 6:1-23 Philippians 3:7-15a	Matthew 7 Hebrews 12:1-14
3d Sunday	9, 71 10, 12	Ezekiel 34:11-16 Jeremiah 2:1-13	Zechariah 1:1-6 Malachi 1:6-14	John 15 I Corinthians 13	Ephesians 4:1-3, 26-32 I Peter 3:1-17
4th Sunday	16, 51 27, 6	Ezekiel 37:1-14 Genesis 5:1-9	Lamentations 1:1-11, 18a Lamentations 3:22-40	John 8:12-18, 25-30 Matthew 16:1-19	Matthew 11:1-6 Matthew 16:21-28

*Responsive reading

199

April

	PSALTER*	OLD TESTAMENT		NEW TESTAMENT	
	MORNING OR EVENING	MORNING	EVENING	MORNING	EVENING
1st Sunday	28, 93 30, 57	Zechariah 9:4-14 Malachi 3:1-6	Exodus 15:1-21 Judges 5:1-5, 31	Mark 2:15-22 Matthew 20:17-29	Matthew 21:33-46 John 10:1-18
2d Sunday	29, 97 33, 43	Isaiah 25:1-9 Exodus 12:21-28, 40-42	Genesis 25:7-11a Exodus 12:43-51	Revelation 5 Romans 5:1-11	Romans 6:4-23 Romans 5:2-21
3d Sunday	34, 99 32, 33	Numbers 23:5-10 Exodus 14:5-22	I Kings 17:8-24 II Kings 19:1-18	I Corinthians 15:12-58 John 6:35-50	II Corinthians 5 Ephesians 2
4th Sunday	11, 145 42, 118	Isaiah 43:1-12 II Samuel 22:1-32	Isaiah 43:13-21 II Samuel 22:33-51	I Thessalonians 4:13-17 Hebrews 11:1-16	Acts 13:46-48 John 12:24-33

*Responsive reading

May

	PSALTER*	OLD TESTAMENT		NEW TESTAMENT	
	MORNING OR EVENING	MORNING	EVENING	MORNING	EVENING
1st Sunday (*Family Sunday*)	128, 82 125, 71	Deuteronomy 33:16-29 Deuteronomy 26:1-11, 16-19	I Chronicles 29:10-15 II Chronicles 7:12-20	John 11:1-46 Acts 10:1-35	Acts 9:36-42 Acts 16:25-40
2d Sunday (*Mother's Day*)	127, 128 113, 66	I Samuel 1:15-18, 20, 24-28 I Samuel 2:1-10	Proverbs 31:1-9 Proverbs 31:10-31	Revelation 7:11-17 Matthew 15:21-28	Matthew 9:18-26 Mark 12:18-27
3d Sunday	116, 112 124, 76	Daniel 7:9-10, 13-14 II Kings 2:1-15	Exodus 24:1-2, 9-18 Deuteronomy 34	Luke 24:13-35 John 21:12-25	Luke 24:36-49 John 20:26-31
4th Sunday	124, 112 122, 93	Isaiah 11:1-9 Joel 2:21-32	Ezekiel 36:16-28 Ezekiel 39:25-29	Matthew 28:16-20 I Corinthians 15:1-14	Acts 1:1-12 Revelation 1:10-18

*Responsive reading

JUNE

| | PSALTER* | OLD TESTAMENT | | NEW TESTAMENT | |
	MORNING OR EVENING	MORNING	EVENING	MORNING	EVENING
1st Sunday	146, 68 104, 42	Genesis 3 Exodus 3:1-14	Genesis 6:1-8, 13-22 Genesis 8:1-4, 15-22	John 14 John 16	Acts 8:1-19 John 17
2d Sunday (*Children's Day*)	147, 23 148, 150	Deuteronomy 31:9-13 I Samuel 3:1-10	Genesis 15:1-18 Exodus 2	Acts 1:1-12 Matthew 18:1-10; 19:13-15	Acts 2 Luke 9:46-48
3d Sunday (*Father's Day*)	112, 84 143 37:29-40	Genesis 48:8-21 Proverbs 4:1-6, 23-27	Genesis 22:1-18 Genesis 25:7-11a	Luke 1:1-17, 57-64, 80 I Corinthians 12:1-12	John 4:46-54 II Corinthians 3
4th Sunday	43, 140 46, 134	Genesis 28:1-5, 10-22 Genesis 32:9-12, 24-30	Exodus 4:18-23a, 27-31 Exodus 6:1-8	Hebrews 1:1-12 I John 1	Hebrews 7:11-25 Hebrews 13:1-8

*Responsive reading

202

July

| | PSALTER* | OLD TESTAMENT | | NEW TESTAMENT | |
	MORNING OR EVENING	MORNING	EVENING	MORNING	EVENING
1st Sunday (*Sunday nearest Independence Day*)	68:1-19 119:20-22, 121, 122	Exodus 13:3-10, 14-22 Isaiah 26:1-15	Judges 6:7-16 Judges 7:2-9	Matthew 22:15-22 Luke 20:9-26	Romans 13:1-7 I Timothy 2:1-13
2d Sunday	5, 28 37:1-11 30	Genesis 37:3-28 Genesis 49:33—50:6, 15-22	Exodus 16:4-15 Exodus 25:1-9	Luke 2:41-52 Acts 3:1-16	Luke 3:1-18 Acts 4:1-22
3d Sunday	37:16-29 40:18 52, 53	Exodus 19:1-11, 16-20a 20:3 Exodus 31:12-18	Exodus 33:1-11 Exodus 33:12-23	Matthew 3:13-17 Acts 5:12-42	Matthew 4:12-25 Acts 6:54-60
4th Sunday	56, 57 37:30-40 40:10-17	Numbers 27:15-23 Joshua 1:1-11, 16-17	Haggai 2:20-23 I Kings 19:13b-21	Mark 2:1-17 Acts 8:1-4, 9:1-22	Mark 3 Acts 9:23-31

*Responsive reading

203

August

| | PSALTER* | OLD TESTAMENT | | NEW TESTAMENT | |
	MORNING OR EVENING	MORNING	EVENING	MORNING	EVENING
1st Sunday	52, 9 13, 8	Job 36:3-7 Job 37:1-14	Job 36:26-33 Job 37:15-24	Matthew 13:1-30 Acts 11:19-30	Matthew 13:31-58 Acts 12:1-17
2d Sunday	73, 33 86, 34	Job 38:1-18 Habakkuk 3:2-15, 17-19	Job 38:19-36 Job 40:1-14	Luke 9:1-17 Acts 13:1-3, 13-16, 38-49	John 6:14-24 Acts 17:13-34
3d Sunday	12, 36 75, 47	Ecclesiastes 3:1-14 Isaiah 63:1-9	Ecclesiastes 7:11-18 Jeremiah 9:23-26	Mark 9:2-13 Acts 18:1-11, 18-23	Mark 9:14-29 Acts 19:21-41
4th Sunday	3, 48 18:1-3, 25-33, 49	Jeremiah 10:1-7 Jeremiah 10:10-16	Daniel 3:28-4:3 Daniel 6:21-23, 25-27	Luke 19:1-10 Acts 20:1-2, 17-38	Luke 18:31-43 Acts 21:3-4, 7-19

*Responsive reading

204

SEPTEMBER

| | PSALTER* | OLD TESTAMENT | | NEW TESTAMENT | |
	MORNING OR EVENING	MORNING	EVENING	MORNING	EVENING
1st Sunday (Sunday nearest Labor Day)	104:23-35 37:1-17 49, 12	Ecclesiastes 5:8-16 Genesis 1:29—2:3	Proverbs 6:6-11 Deuteronomy 24:14-15, 17-22	Matthew 20:1-16 Acts 26:32—27:1-2, 9-25	II Thessalonians 3:10-16 II Timothy 4:9-18
2d Sunday	94, 41 119:33-48 37:18-28	Ecclesiastes 11:1-8a Deuteronomy 15:7-11	Ecclesiastes 4:4-12 II Samuel 24:18-24a	Luke 16:19-31 I Corinthians 13	Luke 16:1-12 I John 3
3d Sunday	119:57-68, 80 119:89-104 42, 13	Isaiah 50:4-10 I Kings 18:21-39	Ezekiel 3:4-11 Ezekiel 3:22-27	Matthew 25:14-29 Romans 12	Luke 19:11-26 Luke 14:1-14
4th Sunday (Christian Education Sunday)	112 119:105-117 25, 19	Deuteronomy 11:13-25 Proverbs 1:7-23	Deuteronomy 13:1-4 Proverbs 9:1-11	John 8:31-43 Galatians 5	John 8:47-59 Luke 14:16-23

*Responsive reading

205

OCTOBER

| | PSALTER* | OLD TESTAMENT | | NEW TESTAMENT | |
	MORNING OR EVENING	MORNING	EVENING	MORNING	EVENING
1st Sunday (*World-wide Communion Sunday*)	111, 11 122, 15	Ecclesiastes 5:1-7 Zechariah 2:1-5, 10-13	Ezekiel 3:1-3 Habakkuk 2	Luke 22:14-30 Ephesians 3:8-21	Matthew 16:20-28 Revelation 2:1-17
2d Sunday	110, 120 48, 14	II Kings 22:3-20 II Kings 23:1-3, 21-25	I Chronicles 28:1-10 I Chronicles 29:1-10	Matthew 28:5-10, 16-20 Ephesians 4:4-24	Luke 22:31-38 Revelation 2:18-29
3d Sunday (*World Order Sunday*)	84, 123 108, 27	Nehemiah 1 Nehemiah 2	Nehemiah 4 Nehemiah 8	John 10:1-18 I Corinthians 12:27 —13:1	Mark 16:14-18, 20 Revelation 3:1-13
4th Sunday (*World Temperance Sunday*) (*Reformation Sunday Last Sunday in October*)	115, 1 119: 1-16	Isaiah 61 Amos 7:7-16a	Isaiah 62:1-7 Amos 8:4-13	John 20:16-23 I Corinthians 1:1-10, 26-31	John 21:1-11 Revelation 3:14-22

*Responsive reading

	PSALTER*	OLD TESTAMENT		NEW TESTAMENT	
	MORNING OR EVENING	MORNING	EVENING	MORNING	EVENING
1st Sunday	61, 112 50, 111	Nehemiah 9:1-12 Numbers 13:1-3, 17-21, 25-33	II Kings 4:38-44 Joshua 5:10-15	Matthew 15:29-39 Hebrews 11:1-16	Luke 17:1-10 Hebrews 13:12-16
2d Sunday	87, 125 106:1-6 47-48 129	Nehemiah 9:13-23 Numbers 14:26-39	II Kings 5:1-14 Joshua 23:1-11	Matthew 15:21-28 Hebrews 11:24-40	Matthew 8:16-27 Revelation 7:9-17
3d Sunday	89:1-18, 145 103, 148	Nehemiah 9:24-38 Numbers 22:1-22a	II Kings 5:15-27 Joshua 24:14-31	Luke 17:11-19 Philippians 4:4-13	Matthew 14:22-36 I Peter 2:1-10
4th Sunday	89, 119:145-160 105:1-8 150	Leviticus 23:1-14 Numbers 24:1-19, 25	Nehemiah 10:28-39 Nehemiah 12:27-31, 38-43	Matthew 8:1-13 II Corinthians 9:6-15	Matthew 9:27-38 Galatians 6:7-10

*Responsive reading

December

	PSALTER*	OLD TESTAMENT		NEW TESTAMENT	
	MORNING OR EVENING	MORNING	EVENING	MORNING	EVENING
1st Sunday	118, 50 97, 46	Isaiah 35 Isaiah 40:1-11	Jeremiah 23:1-8 Jeremiah 31:1-12	Luke 1:1-17 Matthew 25:31-46	Ephesians 1:1-12 II Peter 3:1-14, 18
2d Sunday (Universal Bible Sunday)	132, 67 138, 75	Isaiah 42:1-17 Daniel 2:31-45	Jeremiah 33:7-16 Zechariah 8:1-8, 20-23	Luke 1:26-38 Matthew 24:4-14	Titus 2:11-14; 3:4-7 Matthew 24:24-31, 36
3d Sunday	93, 98 144, 97	Isaiah 52:1-10 Isaiah 28:1-16	Ezekiel 16:22-24 Isaiah 30:8-21	Matthew 1:16, 18-25 Matthew 24:38-51	Luke 11:46-55 I Thessalonians 5:1-11
4th Sunday	126, 9 145, 96	Isaiah 44:1-8, 21-23 Isaiah 49:1-13	Isaiah 66:10-24 Malachi 4	John 1:1-14 Revelation 22	II Timothy 3:1-5, 14—4:8 4:8 I Thessalonians 4:14-18

*Responsive reading

THE HOLY COMMUNION OF THE LORD'S SUPPER
MORNING OR EVENING

THE PSALTER RESPONSIVE READINGS	OLD TESTAMENT	NEW TESTAMENT
15	Exodus 12:1-14	Mark 14:17-26
23	Numbers 9:1-8	John 6:51-58
24	Deuteronomy 16:1-8	Acts 2:36-47
26	II Chronicles 30:13-20	I Corinthians 11:23-29
51	Isaiah 56:1-8	Hebrews 10:1-22
63	Jeremiah 31:31-35	I John 3

YOUTH SUNDAY
MORNING OR EVENING

THE PSALTER RESPONSIVE READINGS	OLD TESTAMENT	NEW TESTAMENT
1	I Samuel 2:18-19, 3:1-10	Matthew 5:3-16
15	I Samuel 9:1-6, 15-17, 15:10, 16-23	Matthew 19:16-22
19	I Samuel 16:1, 4-14 II Samuel 7:4, 8-9, 14-17	Luke 2:41-52
23	Ecclesiastes 11:9 — 12:7, 13-14	Luke 15:11-32
27	Proverbs 1	I Timothy 4:12-16
119:1-16	Proverbs 2	II Timothy 1:1-10, 13-14
119:33-39, 57-64	Jeremiah 1:4-10	II Timothy 2:1-6, 22-23

PALM SUNDAY
MORNING OR EVENING

THE PSALTER RESPONSIVE READINGS	OLD TESTAMENT	NEW TESTAMENT
8	Isaiah 51:8-18	Matthew 26:1-16
23	Isaiah 59:1-2, 16-21	Matthew 27:11-29
24	Jeremiah 7:1-14	Mark 11:1-11
62	Jeremiah 8:9-15, 18-22	Luke 19:29-44
97	Zechariah 9:9-17	Philippians 2:5-11
138	Malachi 3	John 12:20-36

GOOD FRIDAY

THE PSALTER RESPONSIVE READINGS	OLD TESTAMENT	NEW TESTAMENT
22	Genesis 22:1-18	Matthew 27:1-61
40	Exodus 12:1-14, 21-28	Mark 15
54	Numbers 21:5-9	Luke 23
69	Isaiah 52:13 — 53:12	John 3:14-21
88	Isaiah 63:1-6	John 27:1-61

EASTER SUNDAY
MORNING OR EVENING

THE PSALTER RESPONSIVE READINGS	OLD TESTAMENT	NEW TESTAMENT
57	Exodus 12:1-14	Matthew 28:1-15
93	Job 14:1-15	Luke 24:1-12
98	Job 19:23-27	John 6:27-47
111	Isaiah 12	John 20:1-10
115	Isaiah 25:1-9	Revelation 14:1-7, 12-13
118	Isaiah 51:9-16	Revelation 22:1-24

PENTECOST SUNDAY (WHITSUNDAY)
MORNING OR EVENING

THE PSALTER RESPONSIVE READINGS	OLD TESTAMENT	NEW TESTAMENT
48	Numbers 11:16-29	John 4:19-24
84	II Chronicles 15:1-15	John 14:16-26
103	Isaiah 11:1-9	John 15:17-27
122	Isaiah 44:1-8, 21-23	Acts 1:1-8
139	Ezekiel 36:22-28	Acts 2:1-21
145	Ezekiel 39:23-29	I John 2:24-29
148	Joel 2:28-32	I John 4:1-13

THANKSGIVING DAY

THE PSALTER RESPONSIVE READINGS	OLD TESTAMENT	NEW TESTAMENT
147	Deuteronomy 8	Luke 12:22-33
65	Deuteronomy 26:1-11	Luke 17:11-19
103	Deuteronomy 32:7-15, 45-47	Romans 4:3, 13-22
107	Joshua 24:1-14	Romans 8:24-28, 35-39
116	I Chronicles 29:9-15, 17-18	Galatians 6:6-10
117	Habakkuk 3:17-19	Colossians 3:1-17

CHRISTMAS DAY

THE PSALTER RESPONSIVE READINGS	OLD TESTAMENT	NEW TESTAMENT
2	Isaiah 7:10-14	Luke 1:46-55
45	Isaiah 9:2-7	Luke 2:1-20
85	Isaiah 11:1-13	Galatians 4:1-7
89:1-37	Micah 4:1-5	I John 4:7-14
132	Micah 5:2-7	I John 4:8-21

END OF THE YEAR (WATCH NIGHT)

THE PSALTER RESPONSIVE READINGS	OLD TESTAMENT	NEW TESTAMENT
16	Deuteronomy 11:1-17	Luke 12:32-48
90	Ecclesiastes 7:8-18	James 5:7-11
103	Ecclesiastes 11	II Peter 3:8-14
121	Isaiah 65:17-24	Jude 14-15, 20-25